Heroines, Rescuers, Rabbis, Spies

Heroines, Rescuers, Rabbis, Spies

Unsung Women of the Holocaust

by Sarah Silberstein Swartz

Second Story Press

Library and Archives Canada Cataloguing in Publication

Title: Heroines, rescuers, rabbis, spies : unsung women of the
    Holocaust / Sarah Silberstein Swartz.
Names: Swartz, Sarah Silberstein, 1947- author.
Identifiers: Canadiana (print) 20220197776 | Canadiana (ebook)
    20220197784 | ISBN 9781772602623 (softcover) | ISBN
    9781772602630 (EPUB)
Subjects: LCSH: Holocaust, Jewish (1939-1945)—Biography—
    Juvenile literature. | LCSH: World War, 1939-1945—Women—
    Biography—Juvenile literature. | LCSH: Jewish women in the
    Holocaust—Biography—Juvenile literature. | LCSH: World War,
    1939-1945—Jewish resistance—Juvenile literature. | LCSH: World
    War, 1939-1945—Underground movements—Juvenile literature. |
    LCSH: Women heroes—Biography—Juvenile literature.
Classification: LCC D804.195 .S93 2022 | DDC j940.53/180922—
    dc23

*Second Story Press gratefully acknowledges the support of the Ontario
Arts Council and the Canada Council for the Arts for our publishing
program. We acknowledge the financial support of the Government of
Canada through the Canada Book Fund.*

 ONTARIO ARTS COUNCIL
CONSEIL DES ARTS DE L'ONTARIO
an Ontario government agency
un organisme du gouvernement de l'Ontario

 Conseil des Arts   Canada Counc
du Canada   for the Arts

Funded by the Government of Canada
Financé par le gouvernement du Canada |  Canada

Published by
SECOND STORY PRESS
20 Maud Street, Suite 401
Toronto, ON M5V 2M5
www.secondstorypress.ca

MIX
Paper from
responsible sources
FSC® C103567

Heroines, Rescuers, Rabbis, Spies

Unsung Women of the Holocaust

Dedicated to my loved ones in the Present:
Ellie Kellman
Rebecca Mira Swartz
Hannah Ruth Swartz

Written for my loved ones for the Future:
Reuben Menachem Swartz
Arlo Silber Moskowitz
Isaac Eagle Moskowitz

In honor of my loved ones from the Past:
Regina Zlotnik Silberstein
Ruth (Zhutah) Zlotnik Altman
Menachem Silberstein

Contents

Introduction

Heroines, Rescuers, Rabbis, Spies: Unsung Women of the Holocaust uncovers the lives and daring deeds of nine brave, resilient women who resisted the Nazis and their racist atrocities. These diverse heroines from different parts of Europe have been largely overlooked with the passage of time. In this book, their powerful stories are told from a feminist perspective and provide a new definition for what it means to be heroic.

These nine unsung heroines of the Holocaust were ordinary women living in extraordinary times—a period of brutal war and genocide in Europe. Many of the women featured in this book were barely out of their teens when they faced difficult choices and decisions for which they were not prepared. Some were at the beginning of their careers as student nurses, journalists, teachers, psychologists, photographers, or spiritual leaders. Circumstances forced them to become smugglers, rescuers, spies, caretakers of orphaned children, and organizers of public soup kitchens.

Jewish women's experiences during the Holocaust differed

from those of men. They were in double jeopardy for their "race" and their gender. At times, they were persecuted more brutally as women than as Jews. They were often raped or coerced into sexual relations in exchange for shelter, food, and their lives. When they became pregnant in the ghettos and camps, Jewish women were forced to have abortions or sent to the gas chambers. Nazi physicians and medical researchers used Jewish and Roma women as subjects for sterilization and other barbarous medical experiments that either killed them or maimed them for life.

While circumcised men were in danger of being physically exposed as Jews, some Jewish women could "pass" more easily as non-Jews. Because they often received a stronger secular education than young men from religious communities, many young Jewish women were fluent in several languages, such as German, Polish, Russian, French, and English—all helpful in dealing with the enemy. In the underground Resistance, women acted boldly as strategic couriers, smuggling weapons, food, medicine, money, and forged documents. Instead of seeing themselves as victims, some risked their lives to become armed fighters alongside men in partisan brigades and other underground Resistance groups. They blew up trains, destroyed bridges and roads, and ambushed Nazi headquarters and confiscated Nazi weapons. The dangers and life-threatening circumstances of the war years gave these audacious young women "equal opportunities" that they might otherwise not have had.

Some Jews remained alive because brave women from different cultures and religions risked their own lives to rescue them. For defying the laws and actions of the Nazi perpetrators and their henchmen, these daring women's stories need to be remembered. Over half the non-Jewish rescuers who have been recognized and honored as Righteous Among the Nations by Yad Vashem, the World Holocaust Remembrance Center in Israel, are women. These more than 12,000 women who saved Jewish lives came from different nations and races. Two Righteous Gentiles who took enormous risks to make ethical choices—Yukiko Kikuchi Sugihara from Japan and Irena Gut Opdyke from Poland—appear in this book.

The nine women in *Heroines, Rescuers, Rabbis, Spies* represent many more heroines who showed courage in struggling against the brutality of the Nazi oppressors. They came from urban centers, country estates, poor villages, and *shtetls*, small towns where a large percentage of the population was Jewish. Some grew up with privilege and wealth, like Vera Rosenberg Atkins; others came from families with little means. Culturally and religiously, some came from traditional Jewish homes, like Faye Lazebnik Schulman and Regina Zlotnik Silberstein. Others were secular and more assimilated into Polish society, like Rachel Eiga Auerbach. Some were well educated and trained in leadership roles, like Rabbi Regina Jonas and Lena Kuchler Silberman. Others, like Ruth Zlotnik Altman, depended on their instincts, sharpened by dangerous circumstances, to make life-and-death decisions. Still others, like Irena Gut Opdyke, who was Catholic, and Japanese Yukiko Kikuchi Sugihara followed values based on their own religion and culture.

With the genocide of six million Jews, many Jewish women were murdered during the Second World War, but some survived to see liberation and life after the Holocaust. Except for Rabbi Regina Jonas, I have chosen to tell the stories of women who out-lived the war—survivors rather than victims. Their defiance of the Nazis' "Final Solution"—total annihilation of Jews—and their determination after the war to overcome their traumatic experiences and painful losses make these women heroines for a second time. Survival itself was a part of their resistance. Their courageous return to postwar "normal" life and their integration as refugees and immigrants in foreign countries are a powerful part of their stories.

I hope that readers will make their own personal connections to the intrepid young women described in this book. Though all the featured heroines have now died—the last one, Faye Lazebnik Schulman, as recently as 2021—I tell their stories, hoping their lives will have an ongoing impact on the next generation. Several of these women were hardly past their adolescence when the war began. Their youth, their brazen courage, their rebellious spirit gave them the indomitable resilience to keep themselves and others alive. As one heroine, Ruth Zlotnik Altman, stated later in her life, "I was fearless and foolish, too young to be afraid." This attitude, combined with the knowledge that life could end at any moment, gave these young heroines the strength to live for a better future, though it was not guaranteed.

The stories in *Heroines, Rescuers, Rabbis, Spies: Unsung Women of the Holocaust*—personal narratives of moral resistance and courage taken from history—can inform our actions today. The daring and compassionate heroines in this book are models for overcoming obstacles, large and small, and standing up against bigotry, hate, and war in today's complex and often unjust world. May these accounts of unsung heroines of the Holocaust inspire the next generation of leaders—young people, regardless of gender, race, nationality, ethnicity, class, or religion—to make their own moral and ethical choices.

Born for the Pulpit

Rabbi Regina Jonas

Born August 3, 1902, Berlin, Germany

Died October 1944, Auschwitz, Poland

For me it was never about being the first [woman rabbi]. I wish I had been the hundred thousandth!

—Rabbi Regina Jonas, February 1939

Who was the first woman to be ordained as a rabbi? When Sally Priesand was given the title in 1972 by the Jewish Reform movement in the United States, she was incorrectly celebrated as the first female rabbi in the world. In fact, it was almost 40 years earlier, on December 27, 1935, that Regina Jonas was ordained—in Berlin, Germany, just as Nazi persecution of the Jewish people was accelerating.

Almost seven years later, on November 6, 1942, Rabbi Regina Jonas was arrested for being a Jew and deported to Theresienstadt concentration camp, where she gave sermons and offered support and comfort to fellow prisoners. On October 12, 1944, she was transferred to Auschwitz-Birkenau death camp, where she was murdered.

After the Holocaust, none of her surviving male colleagues from the Berlin Jewish Community of the 1930s and 1940s ever mentioned her ordination, her achievements, or even her name. This included the notable Berlin rabbi Leo Baeck, liberal spokesperson for German Jewry before the war and a fellow prisoner in Theresienstadt. Not only had he been one of her teachers, but he had signed a German translation of her Hebrew rabbinical diploma in 1941, just before he was deported. Why then—after he survived the Holocaust and she did not—did he fail to tell the world about her?

It seemed that Regina Jonas's story—as a heroine who fought for a woman's right to become a rabbi and as an unwavering leader in the Jewish community during catastrophic times—had been erased by the Holocaust. Only in the late 1990s, after the fall of the Berlin Wall and the reunification of East and West Germany, were her achievements finally rediscovered and honored.

The Legacy of German Jewish Feminism

The Nazis not only curtailed Rabbi Regina Jonas's groundbreaking career but also interrupted the beginnings of Jewish feminism in Germany. We will never know how many women might have followed in her footsteps sooner had the Holocaust never happened.

The Jewish feminist movement began in Germany in the early twentieth century. In 1904, feminist reformer Berta Pappenheim fought for women's rights and equality in the German Jewish community and established the *Jüdischer Frauenbund* (League of Jewish Women). Under her guidance, the League provided women with career training and feminist education and supported unwed mothers, illegitimate children, and sex workers. It also tried to expand women's leadership roles within the Jewish community. Within its first ten years, the *Frauenbund* had a membership of 35,000 Jewish women. In 1939, it was disbanded by the Nazis.

By the time Regina Jonas began studying to become a rabbi, the growing Jewish Reform movement in Germany was already attempting to combine traditional Judaism with contemporary European life. In progressive synagogues, women were no longer hidden behind curtains or banished to the balcony. There was a new and growing awareness of gender inequality in ritual, prayer, and education.

Educational opportunities in Jewish studies were opening for girls and women. And for the first time, young Jewish girls were being celebrated. The first recorded synagogue coming-of-age ceremony for girls was held in Berlin at the Beer Temple in 1817. A letter documents that the rabbi "blessed two daughters of Jewish parents in the splendid Beer Temple…in an extremely ceremonial manner. A gathering of 400 people, as many as the Temple could accommodate, dissolved…into tears." As liberal Judaism developed a greater following, there were more ceremonies for girls, including synagogue confirmations at which young girls of 12 or 13 were blessed and accepted as members of the Jewish community. In 1917, at the Orthodox Rykestrasse Synagogue in Berlin, the progressive rabbi Dr. Max Weyl supported Jewish education for girls and women and led the girls' section of the Jewish religious school. He also introduced the ritual of bat mitzvah to his congregation. This was five years before American Judith Kaplan, the daughter of Mordecai Kaplan (founder of the American Reconstructionist movement), had her bat mitzvah in New York City in 1922.

It isn't known whether Regina Jonas had a bat mitzvah, but individual bat mitzvah ceremonies did take place in Berlin, even after the Nazis came to power in 1933. A certificate dated 1936 shows that Alice Redlich was called to read from the Torah at an egalitarian synagogue on Prinzregentenstrasse, where women and men were seated together. In the certificate, the word *Knabe* (boy) is crossed out by hand and replaced by *Mädchen* (girl). Stories told by Holocaust survivors confirm that Jews in Berlin were not afraid to innovate and celebrate in resistance to the brutal Nazi persecution happening to them.

The Road to Ordination

I was born in Berlin to a religious family and my father died when I was 11 years old. I didn't have the means to go to university, but I studied hard at the Institute for the Study of Judaism.

—Rabbi Regina Jonas

Regina Jonas, the first ordained female rabbi in the history of Judaism, was born on August 3, 1902, the second child of Sara (Hess) and Wolf Jonas. Unlike many German Jewish feminists of the period, Jonas did not come from a distinguished, wealthy family. She was brought up in a religious home in a poor, working-class Berlin neighborhood called Scheunenviertel. Scheunenviertel was mostly inhabited by *Ostjuden*, religious Yiddish-speaking Jews from Eastern Europe, many of whom had fled anti-Semitism and pogroms. In this section of the city, apartments were often overcrowded, and several families shared a toilet located in the hallway or backyard. The Jonas family moved often from one dwelling to the next. When he died prematurely, her father received a third-class burial, paid for in installments by his wife, because that was all that the family could afford.

Trained as teachers, both her parents believed in education, and as a child, Regina thrived within her family and her Jewish environment. Though they were religious, her parents were modern for their time, giving their daughter only the Latin name "Regina," rather than a biblical or Hebrew one after a deceased relative, as was the Ashkenazi Jewish custom. Her father proudly became her first teacher of religious education. It was probably because of his inspiring influence that Regina wanted to be a rabbi from a very young age. Even after his death in 1913, young Regina continued to study Jewish subjects. Her early classmates remembered that she always wanted to be a rabbi. Later, in 1935, her mother told a journalist who was covering the story of Rabbi Jonas's ordination that, even as a little girl, Regina behaved like a leader, influencing her classmates.

After her father's death, Regina, her mother, and her older brother moved to Prenzlauer Berg, a more affluent section of Berlin, where her mother often took her children to services at the nearby Rykestrasse Synagogue. This synagogue, where the progressive rabbi Max Weyl often officiated, combined tradition and liberal Judaism. When Regina was old enough, she attended the *Jüdische-Mädchen Mittelschule* (Jewish Girls' Middle School), studying

9

Hebrew, religion, and Jewish history. Recognizing Regina's talents, Rabbi Weyl became her mentor, and she studied rabbinic literature privately with him each week for many years, even after her ordination.

After graduation from middle school, Regina spent a short time at an academic prep school, where she received a teaching certificate. This gave her a profession and some financial independence. Teaching Hebrew and religion in various schools, Regina now had the funds to enter the *Hochschule für die Wissenschaft des Judentums* (Institute for the Study of Judaism), Germany's liberal rabbinical seminary, which specialized in teaching students to interpret and argue Jewish texts. Unlike the Orthodox seminary, the Institute allowed women to attend classes, even though it ordained only male rabbis. In a 1932 class of 155 students, 27 were women. Among them, Regina Jonas was the only woman who aspired to become a rabbi.

For her final graduation thesis, Regina chose the topic "Can Women Serve as Rabbis?" Her 88-page paper argued that women could hold rabbinic office. On the first page, she wrote that she personally "loved this profession" and wanted to practice it. She concluded the paper, "Almost nothing halakhically [legally], except for prejudice and unfamiliarity, stands against women holding rabbinic office." Hers was the first attempt to use *halakhah*, Jewish law, to argue for women's ordination. Backing up her argument with biblical sources, she wrote that the question of ordaining a woman was based on historic tradition rather than Jewish law. Her paper was accepted by Eduard Baneth, the supportive professor responsible for the Institute's ordinations. His sudden death—less than a month after he had accepted Regina Jonas's paper and exam results—delayed her hope of receiving official ordination. Steeped in controversy over the question of female ordination, the Institute for the Study of Judaism rejected her appointment as a rabbi because she was a woman. When she graduated from the Institute in 1930, it was as an academic teacher of religion. It would be another five years before she would receive ordination.

Meanwhile, Regina Jonas taught religious studies in Jewish and public schools. She was a popular teacher, especially with young girls. She enthusiastically shared her deep knowledge of Judaism and, according to her students, she was amusing, down to earth, and loved to laugh. Though she was serious about what she taught, she was never strict with her pupils. She also inspired adults with her lectures on such topics as the important roles of women in Judaism.

Regina Jonas was a talented speaker and interpreter of Jewish customs, history, and law. In addition to support from her mentor Rabbi Weyl, she received encouragement from several of Berlin's other rabbis. One of them, Rabbi Isidor Bleichrode, was dedicated to the religious training of young people, male and female alike, even though he was Orthodox. As rabbi of the Kottbusser Ufer Synagogue and rector of the Annenstrasse religious school, he hired Regina Jonas as a teacher. She gave lectures to his congregation, including one called "Youth and Prayer." After the lecture, Regina was clearly pleased. She wrote, "Dr. Bleichrode is impressed by the applause—they all wanted to be my student."

Beginning of a Rabbinic Career

I hope a time will come…in which there will be no more questions on the subject of "woman"; for as long as there are questions, something is wrong.

—Rabbi Regina Jonas

Regina Jonas wanted to do more than teach. She wanted to be a leader. To achieve this goal, she continued her rabbinic study and persisted in pursuing ordination. Though she continued to attend lectures and seminars at the Institute for the Study of Judaism, she was repeatedly denied ordination. Ordination of a woman rabbi remained controversial in the Jewish mainstream. She finally consulted with a circle of liberal academic supporters about the possibility of *semikhah*, private ordination. On December 27, 1935, Rabbi Max Dienemann, director of the Association of Liberal Rabbis, gave her an oral exam and presented her with a rabbinic diploma. She had finally achieved her childhood dream: to become the first ordained woman rabbi.

In spite of her new title, Berlin's Jewish male leadership did not give her the opportunity to lead services nor to preach from the synagogue pulpit. Documents show that she applied for employment at Berlin's progressive Neue Synagogue on Oranienburgstrasse but was turned away. Unable to obtain a pulpit position, she continued to teach and lecture.

She found support from the League of Jewish Women, which gave her the opportunity to work as a chaplain in various Jewish social institutions. She gave lectures to other Jewish women's groups, such as the WIZO (Women's International Zionist Organization) and the sisterhood of B'nai Brith. Over time, more of her lectures were on topics of women's emancipation and Jewish women's issues in the German Jewish community. In the purple robe she wore to distinguish herself from her male counterparts, she continued to preach and teach. When the Nazis banned Jewish education in Berlin schools, Jonas invited young girls to study with her in her own apartment. Just as she had fought for her position as a rabbi, she worked tirelessly to promote equality for Jewish girls and women. She became their role model.

Finally, in 1937, almost a year before *Kristallnacht*, the established Berlin Jewish Community officially granted Rabbi Regina Jonas the title of pastoral-rabbinic counselor. Pastoral care—working with the young, the elderly, the sick, and the neglected—was less prestigious for rabbis than teaching and preaching. But Rabbi Jonas, raised in Scheunenviertel surrounded by poverty, wanted to help the needy Jews of the community and give them spiritual comfort during the darkening times. In this role, she ministered to people in Jewish welfare institutions, such as the Jewish Hospital and the Jewish Home for the Elderly. With daily visits, she offered them solace. She also spent time in institutions for the disabled and with inmates in a German women's prison.

The situation for Jews in Germany was changing. The Jewish community, now under the auspices of the Nazi regime, assigned her to lead services in small Jewish communities outside Berlin. She traveled to such German cities as Bremen, Braunschweig, Göttingen, Frankfurt am Oder, Pommern, and Wolfenbüttel, places that by this time had lost their own spiritual leaders to exile or imprisonment by the Nazis. Her compassion, her education, and her skills as a leader were finally being utilized.

In Nazi Europe

The Nazi Party had come to power in Germany in 1933 with Adolf Hitler as its leader. In 1935, the year of Rabbi Regina Jonas's ordination, the Nazis issued the Nuremberg Race Laws against the Jews. These laws dissolved German citizenship for Jews, took away their religious rights, and restricted both Jewish education and public education for Jews. Hitler expanded his anti-Semitic racist laws to ban Jews from interacting in public. After *Kristallnacht*, the German countrywide pogrom of November 9, 1938, it became obvious that there was no future for Jews in Germany. The Jewish population in Berlin began to shrink. Those Jews who had the means emigrated. Many of those who couldn't emigrate were forced into hard labor or deported to concentration camps. Hundreds of rabbis fled Germany or were imprisoned. Jonas's mentor, Rabbi Weyl, was deported to Theresienstadt concentration camp, and Rabbi Dienemann was interned in several concentration camps before finally escaping to London, England. Rabbi Bleichrode left Berlin for Jerusalem.

Many people advised Rabbi Jonas to leave Nazi Germany while she could. But she rejected the idea of leaving her people behind. It was more important to her to stay with those who needed and trusted her than to save her own life. Her decision to support those afraid and suffering in Berlin, and later in Theresienstadt, became her ultimate defiant act of resistance and leadership.

As more rabbis fled, Rabbi Jonas was asked to head services at established liberal synagogues in Berlin, such as the Kottbusser Ufer Synagogue and the Neue Synagogue. Gender conventions were suddenly dropped in these dire circumstances. Her opportunity to lead a congregation had finally arrived! The more that Jews were persecuted, the greater was their need to embrace Jewish culture, religion, and history. This was Rabbi Regina Jonas's chance to contribute what she had learned with her usual compassion and grace. In a time of overwhelming evil, Rabbi Regina Jonas taught Judaism with joy and passion to the young, the old, the sick, and the dying.

◊◊◊

In Berlin, there were no ghettos. Instead, Jews were forced into *Judenhäuser*, Jewish houses, where several families lived in apartments, one room to a family. In the winter of 1940–41, Regina and her mother were forced out of their apartment and transferred to a *Judenhaus* that they shared with other families. By spring 1941, the remaining 55,000 Jews in Berlin were forced to work in war-related enterprises. In May 1942, Rabbi Regina Jonas was assigned to forced labor at a factory that produced cardboard boxes. In the evenings, she secretly continued to conduct prayer services.

On November 6, 1942, she and her mother were deported to Theresienstadt, a "model" concentration camp set up as a Jewish town—the showplace the Nazis used to lie to the world about what they were doing to the Jewish people. Once in Theresienstadt, Jonas kept up her work, counseling fellow prisoners, providing them with guidance and comfort, preventing suicides, and giving uplifting sermons. Allowed some freedom to live a cultural life in Theresienstadt, Jews formed a lecture circuit and gave more than 2,000 lectures to the prisoners. Some of those lectures were given by Rabbi Regina Jonas.

A list of her handwritten lectures exists today in the Theresienstadt Archive under the title "Lectures of the Only Female

Rabbi, Regina Jonas." It includes the titles of 24 lectures on Jewish holidays, Jewish beliefs and ethics, themes from the Bible and the Talmud, and the history of Jewish women. Five of the 24 titles deal with Jewish women. The archive also includes a poster advertising "Lectures by the Only Female Rabbi, Regina Jonas."

As the Russian army approached and the defeat of Nazi Germany became inevitable, the Nazis accelerated their effort to achieve their goal of Jewish genocide. Beginning in September 1944, more trains left Theresienstadt for Auschwitz death camp. One of the last transports from Theresienstadt to Auschwitz left on October 12, 1944. Rabbi Regina Jonas, age 42, and her 68-year-old mother were prisoners on this train.

Rediscovering Rabbi Regina Jonas

I came to my work out of the religious belief that God is not an oppressor; therefore, man does not control woman, nor does he hold spiritual supremacy over her. I came to this from the belief in the absolute and complete spiritual, psychological, moral equality of the sexes.

—Rabbi Regina Jonas

In Theresienstadt, Jonas had worked closely with Victor Frankl, a prominent Jewish psychiatrist from Vienna who survived the Holocaust. Working together in the Theresienstadt "department of health and hygiene," they greeted the newly arriving Jews at the train station and helped them adjust to their limited new lives. Though Frankl often spoke after the war about his own experiences in Theresienstadt, he never mentioned Rabbi Regina Jonas or her leadership role during their two years as fellow prisoners. Like Rabbi Leo Baeck, he failed to refer to her achievements and the importance of her leadership in Berlin and Theresienstadt. Nor did he mention her legacy as the first woman rabbi. It took more than 50 years for the world to rediscover her.

In 1942, when Rabbi Jonas realized she would soon face deportation, she placed 14 files of documents with the Berlin Jewish Community for safekeeping. The original official documents of her ordination, a copy of her essay "Can Women Serve as Rabbis?" and two photos in her rabbinic robes were part of the collection, along with other documents she had selected, including hundreds of her writings, certificates, manuscripts, letters, postcards, articles, and official notices from the Jewish Community of Berlin. Perhaps she knew she had to save her own place in history.

Her collection of documents was passed on to the Central Archive of German Jewry controlled by the Nazis, who kept them to document the "vanished Jewish race" in Europe. After the war, Soviet officials in East Germany transferred these documents to the German Central Archive, where they lay unexamined for another 50 years. Thus, Rabbi Regina Jonas remained one of the many heroic women—and the first ordained woman rabbi—written out of Holocaust history.

After the fall of the Soviet Union and the reunification of East and West Germany, scholars from around the world uncovered many documents in abandoned archives that had been held by the German Democratic Republic (GDR), the communist state of East Germany. In 1991, Katharina von Kellenbach, a German feminist scholar of religion, was researching German women who had sought religious ordination in the 1930s. She discovered an envelope containing a document in German and Hebrew that showed Jonas's name on a teaching certificate. Continuing her research, she found all of Jonas's files. She, and later other feminist scholars, examined the treasure trove now at the *Gesamtarchiv der deutschen Juden* (the Collected Archive of German Jews) in Berlin, where Jonas's documents were eventually placed. In 1999, Rabbi Elisa Klapheck brought international attention to Rabbi Jonas with the publication of a biography, *Fräulein Rabbiner Jonas: The Story of the First Woman Rabbi*, which included Regina Jonas's 1930 treatise "Can Women Serve as Rabbis?"

In June 2001, as Rabbi Regina Jonas's groundbreaking place in history was finally acknowledged, an international delegation of feminist rabbis, scholars, and communal leaders assembled to unveil a plaque honoring Jonas at her last home in Berlin. The delegation included rabbis from many Jewish denominations and countries, including the first women rabbis to be ordained in the Reform, Conservative, Reconstructionist, and Orthodox communities. From Berlin, they traveled to the Czech Republic and visited Theresienstadt where another memorial plaque to Rabbi Jonas was unveiled.

Today there are over a thousand female rabbis who represent Jewish communities around the world. With each one, Rabbi Regina Jonas's legacy continues.

Woman Warrior with a Camera

Faye (Faigel) Lazebnik Schulman

Born November 28, 1919
Died April 24, 2021

I want people to know that there was [Jewish] resis-
tance. Jews did not go like sheep to the slaughter. I
was a photographer. I have pictures. I have proof.

—Faye Schulman

The year is 1995 and Faye Schulman is giving a presentation on a big screen at the Jewish Community Centre in downtown Toronto. It includes a slideshow of her partisan photographs taken during the Second World War in White Russia/Belorussia (today Belarus), which was part of Poland at that time. The full-capacity audience listens attentively to Faye's talk, mesmerized by the stunning images from another time, another place, a haunting past reality. Some people in the audience may have heard or read stories about partisan fighters during the Second World War—even Jewish Resistance fighters. But the beautifully composed, high-quality photographs of partisan life in the forests and swamps of Belarus being shown bring these fighters' accounts to life.

Faye's poignant images show long trenches filled with corpses of Jewish people murdered by the Nazis. She documents a joint funeral where Jewish and Christian partisans are about to be buried side by side in one grave. There are shots of her and others tending the wounded in the woods, assisting in surgeries on makeshift operating tables made from tree branches. Other pictures record their rifle practice in the woods. They are a powerful testimony of

Jewish resistance during the Nazi atrocities.

Faye Schulman's personal story of Jewish resistance is as remarkable as her photographs. She spent almost two years in the forests of White Russia with the Soviet Molotov Brigade—often the only female guerilla fighter on a mission. In 1995, *A Partisan's Memoir: Woman of the Holocaust* had just been published. It is the first-person account of her determination to avenge the murder of her family members. Having sought vengeance during the war, her goal *after* the war was to remind people to never forget.

Faye Schulman was a Jewish woman warrior—a courageous eyewitness to Jewish armed resistance during the years of the Holocaust. Many years later, she opened others' eyes, young and old, to the reality of her experiences with her astonishing photos and stories. She was one of the few, if not the only, embedded female Jewish photographers to chronicle in real time the experience of Resistance fighters during the Second World War.

Jewish Roots in Polish/Russian/Nazi Belorussia

Lenin, the Polish town of my birth, stood on the shore of the Sluch River. On the other side of the river was the Soviet Union. A scrupulously guarded bridge, the only bridge for many kilometers, separated the two countries. Even before the beginning of the Second World War, the townspeople had been forbidden to approach the river, which served as a border.

—Faye Schulman

Born Faigel Lazebnik, Faye was the fifth child of Rayzel (Migdalovich) and Yakob Lazebnik. Though a failed businessman, her father was a respected member of the Jewish community and an administrator for the local synagogue. Her mother, who provided for their seven children, ran a catering business from their house. Faigel's family consisted of four brothers and three sisters in a traditional Yiddish-speaking Jewish home. Before the war, the Lazebnik family lived a peaceful life in the *shtetl* of Lenin, a small Polish town bordering Soviet Russia. According to her, Jews and Christians in Lenin had good relations before the Holocaust. The town had only one church but two synagogues. Before the Holocaust, Lenin had a Jewish population of about 5,000 to 6,000, half its inhabitants. The other inhabitants were mostly Christian White Russians who spoke the Belarussian language and identified more with Russia than with Poland.

Faigel's older brother Moishe was a trained photographer who ran a portrait business in several towns near Lenin. He taught Faigel, from the time she was ten years old, to take professional photographs and to develop and print them. She learned how to tint black-and-white portraits with color, a common practice at that time. It was a lucrative business. By 16, Faigel was an independent teenager with a successful profession who ran much of her brother's business. The skills and self-reliance she learned at a very young age would later save her life.

Faigel grew up speaking Yiddish at home, learned Polish in school, and spoke fluent Belarussian and Russian in the streets. Regions in White Russia, also called Belarussia, frequently changed hands during the twentieth century. (*Bela* means "white," thus White Russia.) Because of its strategic border location, the town was always protected by the military, regardless of which country it belonged to at the time—Poland, Soviet Russia (also called the Soviet Union, the USSR, or the Union of Soviet Socialist Republics), or Nazi Germany. After Germany and Soviet Russia signed a treaty with each other in August 1939, the Nazi-Soviet Non-Aggression Pact, the Soviet army occupied eastern Poland, including the town of Lenin. Later, the Nazis went to war with Soviet Russia and invaded the region. After the Second World War ended, the town of Lenin became part of the Belarussian Republic of the USSR, until its demise. Today, the region is in the independent country of Belarus.

When the town of Lenin fell under Soviet control, the situation was no worse for Lenin Jews than for their Christian neighbors. But on June 22, 1941, Nazi Germany declared war on Soviet Russia, and eastern Poland went from Russian to Nazi control. On June 24, 1941, the Germans took control of the town, and Nazi anti-Jewish laws were imposed on the citizens of Lenin. First the Nazis looted Jewish possessions. Then they confiscated Jewish stores and businesses, and declared that Jewish children were no longer allowed to attend public schools. Soon after, Jewish homes were taken over by the Nazis, and most adult Jewish men, including Faigel's two older brothers, were deported to a forced labor camp in nearby Gancevich.

On May 10, 1942, Lenin's remaining Jews were forced into a ghetto covering a two-block area. Food became scarce. When Jews in the ghetto were required to work without pay, Faigel cleaned Nazi houses that had previously been owned by Jewish families. Eventually, she was allowed to continue working at her profession, photographing Nazi officials and developing prints to satisfy their obsessive record-keeping.

Faigel was given a special permit to leave the ghetto to enter her family's former house, where her darkroom for developing prints was still located. Once outside the ghetto, she would secretly barter with farmers, exchanging clothing from the ghetto for bread, potatoes, and grain. She then snuck the food back into the ghetto to share with her family and others.

On August 14, 1942, Jewish life in Lenin ended. The Nazis rounded up all the Jews from the ghetto, crowded them into open trucks, and brought them to three long trenches that had been dug outside the town line. There, 1,850 Jews from the Lenin ghetto were shot to death—including Faigel's parents, her two sisters, and her younger brother—and buried in a mass grave. The Nazis took photographs of the mass graves.

Because the Nazis required their skills, 26 Jews were spared from the Lenin massacre, among them a carpenter, a shoemaker, a tailor, a blacksmith, and a painter. These "useful" Jews were imprisoned in the local synagogue before the massacre and were released only when they were needed. As a photographer, Faigel Lazebnik was one of the "lucky" ones whose life was spared because of her special skills. Though Faigel's camera was confiscated, she was still permitted to visit her former family house to develop the Nazis' photographs.

Among the Nazi photos she was ordered to print were the images taken during the Jewish massacre in Lenin. When she printed the photos of the mass graves filled with corpses, she recognized the faces of her murdered family members. Though she was devastated, she was alert enough to secretly keep copies of the prints, despite the serious danger this posed. Those prints were proof of the Nazi genocide of the Jews, which she would show to the world five decades later.

In the Forest

Mourning her family and her community, Faigel escaped alone from Nazi-occupied Lenin as soon as she could. During a raid on the Nazis in Lenin a month after the massacre, she fled with the attacking Russian partisans to the surrounding forests. The Molotov Brigade, which had organized the raid, was a guerilla fighting unit made up of escaped Russian prisoners, part of a larger network of 2,000 Soviet citizens from different backgrounds headquartered in Moscow. The brigade was named after the Soviet leader Molotov, who had signed the Nazi-Soviet Non-Aggression Pact. Many were former Russian soldiers, prisoners of war who had escaped from Nazi prison camps. The unit's camp was located deep in the forests, along the rivers and swamp land of Polesie, between Lenin and Pinsk.

Just as she had saved her own life by persuading the Nazis to give her special privileges, so too did Faigel convince the partisan commander to accept her into the Molotov Brigade. Faigel—now going by her Slavic name, Fanya—did not admit that she was Jewish. Out of approximately 200,000 Resistance fighters in Eastern Europe, about 20,000 to 30,000 were Jews. Though many Jews fled into the woods when their lives were endangered, they were often rejected by the partisans because of anti-Semitism or because they were accompanied by children. Many escaped Jews who were not admitted into a partisan unit lived in the woods, cold, hungry, but alive, in Jewish "family camps."

But if a Jew was single and had guns or former military experience, they were more likely to join the Russian Soviet guerilla units. With no gun and no military experience, Faigel needed to find other reasons to be accepted by the male Russian partisan leaders. She spoke Russian fluently, with no accent, and knew Belarussian and Polish. She told them about her skills as a photographer. She lied that she had some medical knowledge because her brother-in-law, recently murdered in the Lenin trenches, had been a doctor. As luck would have it, this last point was very attractive to the camp leaders. Their only doctor was a trained veterinarian who needed a nursing assistant. As a woman, she was readily accepted as a nurse and became one of the few women in their partisan unit.

A quick learner, Faigel trained to be a nurse with the veterinarian, Ivan Vasilievich. He became her mentor and protector. At first, her job was to wash and change used bandages and clean infected wounds. She also learned to sew skin together and remove bullets from flesh, using vodka as an anesthetic. She treated wounded and sick partisans for gangrene and typhoid fever. Eventually, she helped with surgeries performed in the open air on primitive operating tables. As a nurse, her chief responsibility was to keep the wounded alive so that they could resume their battle against the Nazis.

Altogether, there were eight women in the Molotov Brigade at various times. It is estimated that women composed only two to three percent of the Soviet partisan movement. Many who volunteered were cooks, scouts, and messengers. Others were intelligence agents or radio operators. Some women became armed fighters on attack missions. Faye would later say that women had to work twice as hard as the men to gain respect from their compatriots.

Life was challenging for all partisans. They often went to

sleep hungry on the cold, wet ground among the trees and swamps. When it was exceedingly cold, they dug underground bunkers to keep themselves warm and away from the rain and the snow. On their attack missions, they often moved far from their base camp. Whenever their camp was attacked, they scattered in smaller groups, forming interim shelters until they could safely return to their base.

Young, fierce, and brave, Faigel became a reliable fighter. With no pillow or blanket, she slept with a rifle under her head. After learning to shoot, she joined guerilla raids on neighboring towns and helped destroy bridges and train tracks used by the Nazis. Very familiar with the local landscape and the neighboring towns, she helped her unit navigate raids between Lenin and Pinsk. Her unit often occupied towns in the region to restock food, medicine, and weapons—or to burn down Nazi headquarters.

Faigel fully accepted her new life as a partisan fighter. During one of the many raids on Lenin's Nazi headquarters, she recovered her beloved camera and photo equipment. She snuck into her family's former house for the last time and asked her fellow partisans to set fire to it, so it could no longer be occupied by the Nazis. After the partisans poured gasoline on the house, she lit the first match. This brought a dramatic end to her previous life.

With camera in hand, Faigel became an embedded photographer, documenting partisan activities in White Russia. She took extraordinary photographs, depicting scenes of partisan detachments, sometimes even during guerilla raids. It was not always easy to manage a camera in the forests, and she often lacked proper photographic equipment. On town raids, she looked for film and the chemicals needed to develop her photos. She often mixed the chemicals herself. In quiet, undisturbed moments, she dried her negatives on a tree branch. When they were dry, she printed the negatives under blankets at night in lieu of a darkroom. During the day, she made sun prints by placing a negative onto light-sensitive photographic paper and holding it toward the sun.

For photos that included images of herself, she prepared the camera on a tripod, adjusting the focus, then looked through the lens to compose the photo. She would then instruct someone else to merely press the button. When she had to move for partisan missions, she wrapped up her equipment and buried her precious camera and tripod at camp to keep them safe. In all, Faigel Lazebnik was able to keep over 100 intimate and revealing photos, documenting the history of underground Resistance during the Second World War.

After Liberation

For me the day of victory was a day of reckoning. Never in my life had I felt so lonely, so sad. Never had I felt such yearning for the parents, family, and friends whom I would never see again.

—Faye Schulman

Faigel/Fanya/Faye Lazebnik Schulman was a partisan for almost two years, from September 1942 to July 1944. When Soviet soldiers liberated Belarussia from the Nazis on July 3, 1944, the Molotov Brigade left the forest and dispersed. Most members went home to their families in different parts of the Soviet Union. Faigel, however, no longer had a home or a family to return to. Her town had been destroyed and, as far as she knew, her entire family had been murdered. During the war, she was in denial about her losses, embracing her life as a partisan. Fighting for vengeance and justice with the partisans gave her something to live for. Now that, too, was gone. Only 24 years of age, she could hardly imagine a future for herself.

When her brigade marched into the center of Minsk for the last time, they were greeted as heroes by Soviet officials and local civilians with music, parades, and flowers. Faye and her fellow partisans received official medals for their bravery. Her former unit commander—now first secretary of the local communist party and head of the Pinsk province—had become her friend. Soviet officials made sure she had food, housing, even a job. She was given work as a news photographer for the largest Pinsk daily newspaper, *Bialoruskaja Pravda*, photographing postwar Eastern Europe. In this job, she took photographs of farmhands and factory workers, party officials, and KGB (Soviet state security) officers—all for the post-liberation Soviet government. As long as she stayed in the Soviet Union, her partisan medal was a badge of honor and a passport.

Still, she felt very much alone in Pinsk, especially with few other Jewish survivors left in the city. She was often in despair over her losses—until she discovered that her older brother Moishe was alive. Moishe, who had taught her everything about photography, was working as a photographer in nearby Minsk. When Faigel found out, she immediately traveled to his apartment, where he lived with a roommate named Morris Schulman.

Before the war, Morris had been an accountant in Warsaw, but had fled eastward to Lenin after Warsaw was occupied and before Lenin was in the hands of the Nazis. Faigel and Morris knew each other from Lenin. During the war, they had briefly seen each other in the forests, where Morris was commander of another partisan unit. When they met in Minsk after the war, they found they had more in common than just Lenin and their partisan experiences. Like many surviving Jews with few remaining relatives and friends, they were both committed to rebuilding a new life after the Holocaust. Suddenly, Faigel *could* imagine a future for herself. Faigel and Morris married on December 12, 1944.

Both decorated former Soviet partisans living in Soviet territory, the couple had all the material things they needed—good housing, plenty of food, and respected jobs. But they were haunted by their past and anxious about their future within the restrictions of the Soviet Union. The Cold War between East and West was beginning, and anti-Semitism lurked around the corner in Eastern Europe. Relations between Soviet Russia and the other Allies were rapidly deteriorating as well. By 1945, the Allies had won the war throughout Europe. The Soviets occupied East Germany, while the United States and the other Allies occupied West Germany.

When Faigel became pregnant, the couple felt even more urgency to secure a safe future for their unborn child. Their goal was to apply for visas to countries outside Europe—maybe Palestine or one in North America. To do so, they had to first seek asylum in West Germany, free from Soviet rule. With no documents other than their medals and Soviet identification papers, neither of which were recognized outside the Soviet bloc, they began a harrowing journey across Eastern Europe. They fled to Poland, through Czechoslovakia and across Austria, until they reached American-occupied West Germany.

There, as Jews, they were admitted to a DP (displaced persons) camp in Landsberg am Lech, in Bavaria near Munich, where they resided for three years, waiting for visas to move abroad. In the Landsberg camp, they lived in the partisan section of the DP camp among others with similar wartime experiences. They joined *Bricha*, an underground movement that illegally brought Jews into British-controlled Palestine. Though Faigel and Morris had considered immigrating to Palestine, after their first child was born in 1946, they wanted a more secure, peaceful life in North America. Canada was the first country to offer them a visa.

New Beginnings in Canada

I live with the past; it's my life.... I would never part with my camera as long as I live. It has so many memories and so many stories. It has seen everything.

—Faye Schulman

In 1948, Faigel, Morris, and their young daughter immigrated to Canada, where Faigel Lazebnik became Faye Schulman. Their first few years in Toronto were difficult. Without personal connections or financial resources, and no English, it was hard to find jobs. They were now poor immigrants, living in one room above a butcher shop. Though he had been an accountant before the war, Morris worked in construction, lifting bricks, until he injured himself. Faye was hired as a sewing machine operator in a factory that made dress shields and shoulder pads. Eventually, Morris was hired by the same factory as a cutter. When they had saved enough money, they bought a hardware store, which they ran for 15 years. In 1993, Morris died. Faye lived for another fruitful 28 years.

◊◊◊

Though she had toiled in a factory as a new immigrant, Faye eventually came back to photography and art, hand tinting black-and-white photographs and painting some of her wartime photo images in oils and watercolor. But her lasting activity was educating people about Jewish resistance during the Holocaust. She used her photographs to illustrate her remarkable story as a Jewish woman partisan.

After the publication of her book *A Partisan's Memoir: Woman of the Holocaust* by a feminist publisher, her reputation as a partisan heroine became better known. She was invited to speak and lecture at community centers, in synagogues, at public schools and universities, and at teachers' seminars, ecumenical gatherings, and commemorative events. She spoke publicly about her Holocaust experiences for decades. Those most affected by her presentations were young people with little or no previous knowledge of the Holocaust. They gravitated toward her.

What was extraordinary about Faye was that she enthusiastically told her powerful story well into her 90s. She was generous and gracious in sharing her narrative and her photos with museums, foundations, filmmakers, and writers. At age 93, Faye agreed to be interviewed by writer Joanne Gilbert for Gilbert's 2012 book *Women of Valor: Polish Jewish Resisters to the Third Reich*. Faye's photographs were on view at the U.S. Holocaust Museum in Washington, DC. More recently, the San Francisco-based Jewish Partisans Educational Foundation organized a traveling and online exhibit of her photographs entitled "Pictures of Resistance: The Photography of Jewish Partisan Faye Schulman," viewed in over 30 cities around the world.

Faye was featured in the 1999 PBS documentary *Daring to Resist* about three Jewish teenage girls who resisted the Nazi reign of terror during the Holocaust. At about the same time, Canadian filmmaker Shelley Saywell accompanied Faye on a return to her hometown of Lenin, now in Belarus, for the first time in 55 years. Saywell's documentary *Out of the Fire* captured Faye's emotional meeting with her Jewish partisan friend Rosa, whom she had not seen since their Molotov Brigade disbanded in 1945. Faye was warmly greeted by the former commander of their partisan group and shared wartime memories at a gathering with other White Russian partisans. In Belarus, the filmmakers were able to locate more photos taken by Faye, not part of her personal collection, in a local partisan museum. At a memorial for Lenin's Jews at the site of the mass graves in Lenin, Faye lit candles and said the *kaddish* prayer for her murdered family.

When her life came to an end at age 101, Faye/Faigel Lazebnik Schulman had accomplished her lifetime mission: keeping true accounts of the Holocaust alive for future generations. Her story and her photographs still appear in books, exhibits, recorded interviews, and films and on websites. As a reminder of all she had experienced and accomplished, she always kept her wartime camera —with its *Doppel Anastigmat* lens and folding bellows—beside her.

Heroine of Six Thousand Visas

Yukiko Kikuchi Sugihara

Born December 17, 1913
Died October 8, 2008

Chiune's Distress
Being undecided
About issuing the visas
Tossing turning contemplating
I hear his bed squeaking all night.

—Yukiko Kikuchi Sugihara

Not many people know the name Yukiko Kikuchi Sugihara, which cannot be found in any official tributes to Holocaust rescuers. She was a poet of Japanese lyrics, a writer, an artist, an amateur musician, and the mother of three sons—all attributes that made her the perfect companion to a Japanese diplomat. But more than that, she was a heroine who stood by her own convictions, even when her own and her children's lives were in danger.

Yukiko's husband was Chiune Sugihara, the Japanese diplomat who is remembered for saving several thousand Polish and Lithuanian Jews during the Second World War. As deputy consul general in Kovno (today Kaunas), Lithuania, he is known to have used his position to issue travel permits to Jewish refugees fleeing the Nazis. While Sugihara was serving in this position, Adolf Hitler, the leader of Nazi Germany, proclaimed the Final Solution to what he called the "Jewish question." The Final Solution was a premeditated plan for the genocide of all the Jews of Europe. In defiance of their own government of Japan, which sided with the Germans, Sugihara and his wife saved thousands of Jewish lives.

Chiune Sugihara, or Sempo as he was called, was a modest man who after the war never spoke about his wartime activities. It was only late in life—when some Jewish survivors whose lives he had saved sought him out—and again after his death that he received many international honors. In 1985, he received the Righteous Among the Nations Award from Yad Vashem, the World Holocaust Remembrance Center in Israel, for saving the lives of Jewish refugees in Lithuania. A grove of cedar trees, called the Sugihara Righteous Forest, was planted just outside Jerusalem in his honor. (This is especially appropriate since *Sugihara* means "cedar grove" in Japanese.)

After his death, the Sugihara House Museum was established in Kovno, where he and his wife, Yukiko, had lived above the consulate. Streets were named after him in Israel, Lithuania, and Brazil. In 2014 in Toronto, Canada, Sugihara was posthumously awarded the Sakura Award by the Japanese Canadian Cultural Centre. A virtual ceremony was hosted by the Embassy of Japan in Canada in December 2020 to commemorate the 120th anniversary of his birth and the 80th anniversary of his issuing visas. In Chestnut Hill, Massachusetts, near Boston, the congregation of Temple Emeth built a Sugihara Memorial Garden and holds an annual Sugihara Memorial Concert in his honor. In Lithuania, 2020 was named the Year of Chiune Sugihara.

But what do we know about Sugihara's wife, Yukiko Kikuchi? Chiune received recognition for saving what some people say were 6,000 Jewish lives, but his wife, Yukiko, was an equal contributor. She risked her life and the lives of their three young children to save the Jews. It was Yukiko who convinced her husband to prepare visas for the hundreds of vulnerable Jewish refugees who came to their door. With every decision about the visas, Chiune asked his wife for her opinion, approval, and support. After his deeds were recognized by the world and he was too ill to travel, Yukiko became his representative, retelling their story and attending the many occasions around the world in which he was honored. She was the unsung heroine behind Chiune's actions.

Background Story

She was born Yukiko Kikuchi on December 17, 1913, in Numazu, Japan. Her father was a progressive high-school principal. Her mother was an educated woman with strong opinions, ahead of her time. According to Yukiko, her mother bought high-heeled shoes as soon as they were first available in Japan. From the age of five, Yukiko wanted to be a poet, and during most of her life, she wrote *tanka*, brief Japanese poems consisting of four or five lines, similar to haiku. She became an independent young woman who didn't want an arranged marriage, as was the custom at the time. Instead, at age 21, she chose to marry Chiune, who had already established his career in the Japanese foreign service. He was 13 years her senior and had been divorced. When Chiune asked her to marry him, he told her it was because she was a confident woman who would be able to adjust to traveling and living in many foreign countries. They were married in February 1935 in Tokyo, where she gave birth to their first son, Hiroki, the following year.

And travel they did. Two years later, they were posted to Helsinki, Finland, where their second son, Chiaki, was born. In Helsinki, they lived an opulent lifestyle in a lovely, large villa. Yukiko enjoyed an active social life as the young wife of a diplomat in peaceful times. She was an elegant hostess and a charming representative of her country. Wearing her beautiful kimonos, she entertained other diplomats and important people, hosting nightly gala dinner parties and tea parties in the afternoon. She learned German and a bit of English to speak with her guests who sometimes numbered over 100. She attracted much attention, and people found the young woman, now in her mid-20s, enchanting and radiant.

The Consulate in Kovno

In November 1939, the Sugiharas' lives changed dramatically. They received a sudden order from the Japanese government notifying them that they would be transferred to Lithuania. A new consulate for the Japanese Empire needed to be opened in Kovno, the capital. Because he spoke Russian and German fluently, Chiune was chosen for the job. At the time, the Japanese government was concerned that fighting might break out between Germany and Russia, two countries that had been allies. Chiune was to report to his Japanese superiors in Berlin and Tokyo on Nazi and Russian troop movements near the Lithuanian borders. The consulate would be a one-person operation, but his superiors allowed his pregnant wife and their children to accompany him.

Between 1920 and 1939, Kovno had been the capital and largest city of then-independent Lithuania. In 1939, it had a Jewish population of 35,000 to 40,000, about one-fourth of the city's total population. Jews were part of the city's commercial, artisan, and professional life. Kovno was a major center of Jewish learning and an important Zionist center. With its rich and varied Jewish culture, it had both Yiddish and Hebrew schools, 40 synagogues, and a Jewish hospital.

Everyday life for the Sugihara family was no longer as grand as it had been in Helsinki. The family lived in quarters on the second floor of the consulate building. They had a small staff who came each day to the Japanese consulate located on the first floor of the building, and two Lithuanian students rented the third floor. There were no more grand parties at the Japanese consulate and no more entertaining foreign guests. Yukiko was pregnant with their third son, Haruki, so her younger sister, Setsuko, joined them in Kovno to help care for the children.

A month after they arrived, the Sugiharas met a young Jewish boy named Solly Ganor in his aunt's grocery store. Solly invited them to join his family and friends at a Hanukkah celebration, where the Japanese couple had a chance to meet people from the

Jewish community. After lighting candles and sharing food on the first night of Hanukkah, the new consul and his wife listened to grim stories of Nazi atrocities in neighboring countries, as told by another guest, a recent refugee from Poland. Their Jewish hosts briefly talked about their fears of Nazi invasion in Lithuania in the coming year. This was the Sugiharas' first contact with a Jewish family in Kovno, and it probably influenced their positive feelings toward their Jewish neighbors.

Yukiko and Chiune had always believed in respecting people of different nationalities and races. In 1935, Chiune had quit his post as deputy foreign minister in Manchuria in protest over Japanese mistreatment of the local Chinese. When Yukiko saw a sign in German—*Jews forbidden!*—at the entrance of a park across from their Kovno house, she was repelled and wrote a tanka poem:

In harsh German
Engraved on cold steel
Proclaimed with an emotionless expression
Jews forbidden.

When the Nazis invaded Poland in September 1939, some Polish Jews fled as refugees to Lithuania, where they hoped they might be safer. Though the Nazis had not yet invaded Lithuania, the Russians were fast approaching from the east. On June 15, 1940, Soviet Russia invaded Lithuania and ordered synagogues and Jewish schools in Kovno to shut down. There were rumors that Nazi Germany and Soviet Russia would soon be on different sides of the war. If the Nazis overtook the Soviets and invaded Lithuania, Jewish lives would be in even greater jeopardy. Options for escape were few, and any attempt to cross international borders required multiple diplomatic permits. The Jewish refugees from Poland and their Jewish Lithuanian counterparts wanted to escape Europe and head to the United States or Canada or British-controlled Palestine, but these countries had strict immigration quotas. The Jews needed exit, transit, and entrance visas to leave war-torn Europe, but no foreign embassy would grant them. The Japanese consulate might be their last hope.

Meanwhile, fearing the future, the still-ruling Soviets ordered all foreign embassies and consulates to be shut down in Lithuania. Chiune was ordered to close the Kovno consulate by the end of the summer.

The "Incident"

The "incident" in Lithuania, as it was later called by Japanese officials, lasted for only one month before the Kovno consulate closed, but it had major repercussions. On the morning of July 27, 1940, nine months after the Sugiharas' arrival, a crowd of frightened Jewish men, women, and children suddenly appeared outside the iron gates of the Japanese consulate. They implored the consul to issue exit and transit visas to help them escape Nazi Europe through Russia to Japan.

Yukiko opened the curtains and looked out the window. On the first day, she saw a group of about 100 men, women, and children in front of the building. Soon the crowd grew to more than 300 people, all pleading for visas. Each day, more people arrived. They waited, day and night, for a response from the Japanese consul. Many were Jews who had escaped from Nazi-occupied Poland, some in horse-drawn carts, others walking for days, until they reached the Japanese consulate in Kovno. They were disheveled, exhausted, and hungry. With no safe haven, they were desperately fleeing for their lives.

Yukiko stood at the window, watching mothers holding crying children in their arms. With three children of her own, she was very upset by what she saw. How could she ignore the desperation in their frightened eyes? Yukiko wrote:

There in a crowd
Waiting for visas

Is a boy
Clutching his father ever so tightly
His face is dirty.

At first, Chiune Sugihara refused to talk to the crowd. He did not want to defy his country's orders. After all, he was an employee of the Japanese Foreign Ministry, and Japan was an ally of Nazi Germany. But more Jewish refugees kept coming each day, and the crowds grew rowdy. A few tried to climb over the fences surrounding the building. Homeless, some refugees slept in the nearby park, waiting for morning. With each passing day, they became more desperate. Chiune consulted with Yukiko and her sister. Both women were adamant about helping the Jews.

Finally, Chiune sent cables to the Japanese Foreign Office, asking for permission to issue visas. Before they were sent, Yukiko copied the cables three times as required. One copy went to the Japanese ambassador in Germany, another to the Japanese ambassador in Latvia. The third and most important cable went to Foreign Minister Yosuke Matsuoka in Tokyo. As he'd expected, all his superiors refused permission, and Chiune Sugihara told the crowd to go away.

But each day there were more refugees who refused to leave. They stood there, tired and frightened, holding small children in their arms. As the crowd grew, Yukiko became more convinced that she and Chiune needed to save these people. He sent another cable to Japan, and then another. But the answer was always the same: *Do not issue visas!*

They agonized. Yukiko and Chiune could not sleep at night. Yukiko was unable to breastfeed her baby because of her anxiety. She knew that Chiune wanted to help the Jewish families. But they had three young children of their own to consider, the youngest only three months old. They knew that if they issued illegal visas to the Jewish refugees, they themselves could face punishment. If Chiune defied his supervisors' instructions and signed the visas, he might lose his job in the foreign service—and his family's livelihood. Or much worse, they and their children might be shot by the Nazis for helping Jews. But 27-year-old Yukiko found it impossible to ignore the many innocent Jewish men, women, and children begging at their doorstep.

Because of the crowds, the Sugihara children had been unable to play in the park across the way. Instead, three-year-old Chiaki and five-year-old Hiroki spent much of their time looking out the windows. Sometimes the Jews would wave their hands and try to make the Sugihara children laugh with funny gestures. Their eldest son, Hiroki, was frightened by the sight of children his own age.

Finally, after much agonizing, they made their decision together—as a family. Ever respectful of his wife's wisdom, Chiune asked for her opinion. Yukiko told her husband that in spite of the risks to their lives, they must help the refugees. Her sister, Setsuko, agreed. Thousands of lives depended on their decision.

Since he could not get Japanese approval, Chiune Sugihara negotiated transit permits with the Soviet Union. These permits would allow the refugees to leave Lithuania to reach the Far East through Russia via the Trans-Siberian Railway. After receiving permission from the Russians, the Japanese consul made an announcement to the crowd outside the consulate. He promised to issue visas to everyone. People cheered and hugged and kissed each other.

Following this announcement, their overwhelming job began. Ignoring official protocol, they worked obsessively, 18 to 20 hours a day, signing countless visas for the refugees to travel to Japanese territory. With Yukiko at his side, Chiune frantically handwrote hundreds and hundreds of visas throughout August. Though Yukiko offered to help, only he could write the official visas. When he became exhausted, Yukiko massaged his arm and urged him to keep signing. Many people were still waiting. "We need to save as many lives as we can," she told her husband. Within a month, they had issued 2,139 visas. These visas may have saved over 6,000 people, since entire families with their children managed to escape on a single visa.

The Sugiharas left Kovno in September 1940, after which the Japanese government reassigned them to Königsberg, Germany, near the Russian border. As they were leaving, more Jewish refugees followed them to the railway station begging for visas. When they ran out of visas, he issued permission papers, blank pieces of paper with his signature and seal, and handed them to the desperate refugees through the windows of the train.

The train pulls away,
Hands reaching out the window
Passing out visas
Hands reaching towards the windows
For visas for life—
HOPE.

On September 27, 1940, Japan signed an alliance with Nazi Germany and Italy, the Tripartite Pact that officially formed the Axis Powers. Shortly thereafter, Nazi Germany instituted the official policy, the Final Solution, that would begin the genocide of the Jewish people in the lands that it conquered. Though Germany requested it, Japan Foreign Minister Yosuke Matsuoka, who signed the Tripartite Pact with Hitler, still refused to institute an official policy of anti-Semitism. He said if he was forced by Hitler to persecute Jews, he would tear up the Tripartite Pact. In an internal memo, he stated that since the Japanese were themselves victims of racism around the world, they would not institute a racist policy.

By spring 1941, most of the Jewish refugees that the Sugiharas had helped arrived in Japan. Their escape had taken them from Lithuania to Russia across 9,600 kilometers (6,000 miles) by Trans-Siberian Railway to Vladivostok, a port on the Sea of Japan and the end point of the Russian railway. From there, they boarded ships to Japan. Most of them reached Japan via Kobe, then went on to Japanese-occupied Shanghai, China, where there was already an established Jewish community. More than 300,000 Jews were allowed to live in peace in Japanese-controlled Shanghai during the Second World War. The Jews who did not manage to escape Lithuania were later murdered by the thousands.

On June 22, 1941, the Nazis invaded Soviet Russia, and the Russian soldiers fled Kovno. In July and August, the Nazis established the Kovno ghetto, where more than 30,000 Jews were imprisoned. One-third were rounded up and taken into the hills where they were shot by German death squads. The rest were sent to concentration camps or death camps. These were the Jews who had not been lucky enough to receive Sugihara visas.

New War Assignments

From Königsberg, Germany, on the Baltic Sea, the Japanese government transferred the Sugiharas to Prague, Bohemia (today the Czech Republic), where Chiune Sugihara became consul general. From there, they were soon relocated to Bucharest, Romania. With each move, the family was given short notice to respond to life-changing events. As the intensity of the war increased, their living conditions worsened and they faced more hardships

Unlike rescuers Oskar Schindler and Raoul Wallenberg, to whom Sempo is often compared, Chiune Sugihara had far less protection, less financial backing, and, most of all, more at stake: the lives of his immediate family. When Japan attacked Pearl Harbor in December 1941 and the United States entered the war against the Axis nations, including Japan, the Japanese government suggested that the families of diplomats leave Europe and return to Japan. But courageous and loyal Yukiko refused to leave her husband's side and remained in ravaged Europe for the rest of the war. In Romania, an ally of Nazi Germany, Yukiko and the children found themselves in a war zone. When the city of Bucharest was attacked by American bombs, the family fled to a cottage in the countryside. Even in the country, the air raids continued, and Yukiko needed to protect her children from the bombings. Though she never suffered the tragedies that she had seen the Jews undergo, there remained many dangers for her and her three young children.

During a 1944 military march through the Balkan countries, Allied Russian soldiers arrested the Sugihara family, along with other diplomats and soldiers from the opposing Axis side. Yukiko, Chiune, and their children became enemy prisoners in a Soviet prisoner-of-war internment camp on the outskirts of Bucharest, where they remained for 18 months.

When they were freed, they made their way back to Japan. Their trip back to their home country took many months. Ironically, they took the same route—the Trans-Siberian Railway—that the Jews had taken, through Siberia and across the sea to Japan. Like the Jews, they stayed in squalid internment camps on the way, often cold, hungry, and covered in fleas and lice.

When they returned to Japan in the spring of 1947, after serving their country for ten brutal years in war-torn Europe, Chiune Sugihara was asked to resign from diplomatic service. He was told it was because of the downsizing of the Japanese Foreign Ministry after its defeat in the war. But the real reason was that he had defied his government's orders by issuing several thousand visas to Jewish refugees. Yukiko later recalled that the Japanese foreign minister told her husband that he was dismissed because of "that incident" in Lithuania.

Honoring the Past

In Japan, the years following the Second World War were difficult for the Sugihara family. Having once lived a luxurious lifestyle, they were now impoverished. Because Chiune had lost his government job, he had to work at menial jobs to support his family. At one point, he sold lightbulbs door to door. Other tragedies followed. Their third son, Haruki, died of leukemia at the age of seven, and later Yukiko's sister also died. In 1949, they had a newborn son, Nobuki, to care for. Later, Chiune began working for an export company. Using his Russian-language skills, he left his family in Japan and moved to the Soviet Union for 16 years. Yukiko, now a single mother, oversaw the household and brought up their sons.

For many years, Yukiko and Chiune had no idea what had happened to the Jews who had received their visas. After the Holocaust, most of them eventually immigrated to other parts of the world—to Canada, the United States, Australia, England, Argentina, Brazil, and Israel. It wasn't until many years later that the Jewish refugees spoke about the Japanese couple that had saved their lives.

In 1968, 28 years after their Kovno experience, they were contacted by an Israeli diplomat, Yehoshua Nishri, stationed at the Israeli embassy in Tokyo. As a Jewish teenager, Yehoshua had run alongside the train as the Sugihara family was leaving Kovno. As the train pulled out, he shouted, "Chiune Sugihara, we will never forget you. I will see you again." He had survived the Holocaust because of a Sugihara visa.

The year after they met Yehoshua Nishri, Chiune and Yukiko visited Israel and were greeted by several other survivors who owed their lives to them. More survivors gathered together and lobbied Yad Vashem, the World Holocaust Remembrance Center, for recognition of the Sugiharas' deeds. In 1985, when Yad Vashem recognized Chiune Sugihara as a Righteous Among the Nations, he was too ill to travel to Israel. Yukiko and their son Hiroki accepted the honor in Jerusalem on his behalf. Chiune Sugihara died the following year in July 1986.

Until her own death on October 8, 2008, Yukiko continued to travel around the world as the family spokesperson. When Yukiko traveled to Jerusalem in 1998, she met survivors who showed her the yellowing visas that she had helped to issue. For over 20 years, she told their rescue story, giving interviews and writing accounts of their experiences during the Second World War. She helped to publicize the deeds of her husband, giving him the credit for what had been their mutual decisions. Yukiko Kikuchi Sugihara became a tireless Holocaust educator, keeping the Sugihara legacy alive.

A photo exhibit, "Visas for Life," was presented in 117 museums worldwide.

There is a Japanese saying: Even a hunter cannot kill a bird that flies to him for refuge. The Sugihara family followed this proverb and, in so doing, it is estimated that as many as 40,000 people living today are descendants of the Jewish asylum seekers who received Sugihara's transit visas.

Chronicler and Conscience
of the Holocaust

Rachel (Rokhl)
Eiga Auerbach

Born December 18, 1903

Died May 31, 1976

These manuscripts have endured much hardship. They were buried in the ground and I...agonized and suffered to bring them once again to the light of day. I succeeded in getting them out of Poland and they came to Israel with me. I brought them in a special box; I never parted from them, neither on the train nor on the boat.

—Rachel Eiga Auerbach

A year after the end of the war in Europe, Rachel Eiga Auerbach was in search of hidden treasures buried deep in the ground. It was September 18, 1946, when—because of her insistence—ten buried metal boxes were uncovered beneath the rubble that had once been the Warsaw Ghetto. They contained documents that reflected the lives and deaths of three million murdered Jews of Poland—historic proof of the genocide perpetrated by the Nazis.

Writer and journalist Rachel Auerbach was one of only three survivors of *Oyneg Shabes*, the group that had collected thousands of pages of accounts from the final years of Jewish life in Poland and hidden them underground for safekeeping. One of the boxes contained Auerbach's own notebooks, including her diary of daily life in the Warsaw Ghetto. The notebooks became her most prized possessions, and she continued to rethink and rewrite them for the rest of her life.

◊◊◊

In 1940, when the Warsaw Ghetto was sealed by the Nazis, the celebrated Jewish historian Emanuel Ringelblum initiated a secret project: collecting Jewish experiences during the brutal Nazi occupation. The Ringelblum Archive went by the code name *Oyneg Shabes* (Yiddish for "the pleasure of the sabbath") because its participants held secret weekly meetings on Saturday afternoons, the Jewish sabbath. Ringelblum summoned writers, teachers, students, economists, and community leaders to record and chronicle everyday Jewish life in Nazi-occupied Poland. Journalist and writer Rachel Auerbach was one of the people he enlisted to join his group of 60 members. Together, the group wrote and collected testimonies, memoirs, letters, posters, leaflets, official announcements, and correspondence in Yiddish, Polish, Hebrew, and German.

As the deportations and killings of the Jewish people became more intense, leaders and caretakers of *Oyneg Shabes* buried thousands of documents for safekeeping. During the first Nazi deportations from the Warsaw Ghetto in August 1942, the first batch of documents was buried in the basement of a Jewish school in the center of the ghetto. A second batch was buried in February 1943 in two sealed aluminum milk cans. Together, the vessels contained about 35,000 pages. When the Ringelblum Archive was recovered after the Holocaust, it became a time capsule of Jewish life in Nazi-occupied Poland—a final testimony recorded in real time by the people who had experienced it. Today, it is considered the most important record of Jewish experiences in Poland during the Holocaust.

Uncovering the buried Ringelblum Archive was the beginning of Rachel Auerbach's courageous mission after the war: chronicling the Holocaust for future generations. A prolific writer and journalist before the war, she became an unwavering activist, demanding that the memories of individual surviving Polish Jews, both important and ordinary people, be painstakingly documented after the war. One of the few female pioneers involved in the early recording of Holocaust history through oral and written personal testimony, Rachel founded the Department for the Collection of Witness Testimony at Yad Vashem, the World Holocaust Remembrance Center in Israel. Her goal was to keep the memory of the Holocaust alive for future generations—in the victims' and survivors' own words.

Yiddish Writer between the Wars

Rachel (Rokhl in Yiddish) Auerbach was born in 1903 in Lanowitz, a *shtetl* in the Polish region of Galicia. She was the daughter of Manya (Kimelman) and merchant Khanina Auerbach, who died in 1924. Her only sibling died in 1935, and her mother did not live long enough to see the Nazi invasion. Before the war, Rachel had a large extended family, but by the time the Holocaust was over, she was its sole survivor.

Rachel combined a deep Jewish cultural identity and a love of Yiddish (the language widely spoken by Jews in Eastern Europe) with a first-class Polish education. Between the First and Second World Wars, the interwar years in which she grew up, Jews were allowed for the first time to attend Polish schools of higher learning. Rachel took advantage of this opportunity. In 1920, her family moved to the urban center of Lvov, then Poland (today Lviv, Ukraine), where she finished high school. She continued her education at the University of Lvov, where she studied history, philosophy, and psychology. After graduation, although certified to teach high-school history and philosophy, she chose a career as a journalist.

While Rachel had a strong Jewish identity, she was never religious. Like many other Jews of her generation, she was more interested in literature, folklore, and other aspects of Jewish culture than in practicing religious Judaism. Rachel was deeply involved in promoting Yiddish language and culture, which she believed should be at the center of contemporary Jewish identity in Eastern

Europe. She believed Yiddish culture could be an antidote for the growing assimilation of educated Jews. To encourage secular Jews to embrace Yiddish language, literature, and culture, she organized local literary salons, public lectures, and conferences.

Rachel Auerbach wrote articles, essays, and literary reviews for the Yiddish press, the Polish Jewish press, and bilingual literary journals in Lvov during the 1920s. She was a founding member and an editor of *Tsushtayer* (Contribution), a Yiddish literary journal that tried to bring educated Galician Jews, who spoke mostly Polish, closer to an appreciation of Yiddish literature and culture. For a time, its editorial office was located in the house of Rachel's parents. She also served as secretary of the Lvov branch of YIVO, the prominent Yiddish cultural institute based in Vilna (today, Vilnius), Lithuania.

In 1933, Rachel moved to Warsaw, then the largest Jewish community in Europe. Warsaw was the hub of Yiddish culture with its dynamic newspapers, literary journals, theater, cabarets, and choirs. It was also the center of Yiddish publishing in Poland. Though she had been a central figure in Lvov Jewish literary circles, Rachel was unable to find full-time work in the male-dominated literary publishing environment in Warsaw. Instead, she worked as a freelance journalist for a variety of Polish and Yiddish newspapers and magazines to make a living. Fully fluent in both Polish and Yiddish, she also worked as a translator from Yiddish to Polish. She became a member of the Association of Jewish Writers and Journalists in Warsaw.

In the pre-Holocaust years, Rachel Auerbach wrote extensively about women's history and literature—as well as gender discrimination. At *Tsushtayer*, she had supported women's literary creativity and encouraged other talented Jewish women writers, such as poets Rokhl Korn and Dvoyre Fogel, to write in Yiddish instead of other languages. Rachel believed that women should be creating literature, rather than merely reading it.

An early feminist in spirit, she addressed the challenges all women faced in creating space for themselves in literature, culture, and society in general. In her essays and reviews, she emphasized the presence of contemporary Yiddish and Polish female writers and noted the history of Polish women writers dating back to the seventeenth century. Unfortunately, these feminist topics, so important to her at that time, were of less concern to her after the tragic events that would follow.

Writing in the Years of the Holocaust

Each day I recall another one of those who are gone.... I feel the need to say Yizkor four times a day...there is a passage recited for those who have no one to remember them and who, at various times, have died violent deaths because they were Jews. And it is people like those who are now in the majority.

—Rachel Auerbach, November 1943

When the Nazis attacked Poland, Rachel considered leaving the country with a group of fellow journalists. In September 1939, just as the Nazis entered Warsaw, she was summoned by Emanuel Ringelblum, who thought highly of both her literary and her managerial skills. He asked her to remain in Warsaw to run a public soup kitchen in the Nazi-occupied city. When she agreed, Rachel Auerbach, the writer, also became a social worker and public activist.

On opening day, her soup kitchen at 40 Leszno Street had 50 visitors. As food became increasingly scarce and the ghetto was closed, that number increased to about 2,000 a day. Most visitors were homeless Jewish refugees driven out of towns and *shtetls* in the Polish countryside. Her soup kitchen also became a destination for starving writers and a meeting place for members of the organized Jewish Resistance. Keeping the doors open as long as she could, Rachel managed the soup kitchen for three years, until the Nazis shut it down.

Running the soup kitchen gave Rachel Auerbach a unique view of the desperate, starving people who visited there each day. In 1941, Ringelblum asked Rachel to join *Oyneg Shabes* and report her daily observations of Warsaw Ghetto life. She wrote a monograph, "A Soup Kitchen in the Warsaw Ghetto," a heart-wrenching picture of the despondent people she encountered daily at the "frontlines of hunger." At night, after grueling 12-hour shifts in the soup kitchen, she would retire to write entries in her ghetto diary. She also documented the rich cultural and literary life that defiantly still existed in the Warsaw Ghetto. She wrote about the Jewish writers, artists, musicians, and actors—the artists and intellectuals whom she had known so well from the interwar years.

In addition, she interviewed and transcribed other people's accounts of the Nazi occupation. One of her most important as-signments for the Ringelblum Archive was to record the testimony of 25-year-old Abraham Jacob Krzepicki, an escaped prisoner from Treblinka, who returned to the Warsaw Ghetto in September 1942. His was one of the earliest firsthand accounts that came out of the Treblinka death camp. Almost 100 typed pages long, his chilling testimony was transcribed into three notebooks, preceded by Rachel's own brief introduction. It became one of the most im-portant documents recovered in the buried Ringelblum Archive.

◊◊◊

A few weeks before the Warsaw Ghetto Uprising and the Nazi liquidation of the ghetto, Rachel fled to the Aryan side of Warsaw. Beginning in March 1943, she lived under the false Polish identity of Aniela Dobrucka. With the support of Christian Polish friends, and aided by her non-Jewish appearance and command of the German language, she worked as a Polish secretary during the day. Walking through the streets of Aryan Warsaw, she sometimes carried a large basket of vegetables, with money and forbidden manuscripts hidden underneath. Whenever she could, she risked her life as a secret courier for the Jewish and Polish Resistance, distributing money and documents to hidden Jews.

But it was paper and ink that became Rachel's most important personal resistance against the Nazis. During the long months of 1943 and 1944, she continued to write on Jewish life in the former Warsaw Ghetto and about the ghetto's destruction. By candlelight, she wrote essays for the underground Jewish National Committee, now secretly relocated on the Aryan side. One essay, "They Called It Deportation," recalled what she had witnessed in the summer of 1942 during the first major roundup of Jews from the Warsaw Ghetto. She also wrote a poetic account entitled "Yizkor, 1943," describing Jewish life in the ghetto and her personal reaction to its destruction. She continued to chronicle the lives and activities of her friends and intellectual colleagues who had been part of the Lvov and Warsaw Jewish cultural communities before the war. By the time she wrote about them, many of them had already been murdered.

Many of the accounts Rachel wrote during her days in Aryan Warsaw were in Polish. They circulated among underground Polish anti-Nazi allies to inform them of the fate of the Polish Jews. She entrusted her later wartime notebooks to her Christian Polish friends Antonina and Jan Zabinski, directors of the Warsaw Zoo in suburban Praga on the other side of the Vistula River, where she herself hid for a short time. Like the Ringelblum Archive, these writings were recovered after the war.

Postwar Jewish "Recovery" in Poland

For Rachel Auerbach, the Ringelblum Archive became even more important after the Holocaust. She was devoted to its legacy. After Warsaw was liberated by Soviet Russian forces, she—one of only three surviving members of the *Oyneg Shabes* group—led the search for the buried archive. Though most traumatized Jewish survivors were more interested in rebuilding their lives than in reexamining the past, she single-mindedly spoke up for the importance of the lost documents and pressured Jewish leaders to search for them. At an early public commemoration of the Warsaw Ghetto Uprising, Rachel—the only woman on the podium—stubbornly insisted that there was a priceless national treasure buried underneath the ruins of Warsaw: "I will not rest and I will not let you rest...until we find it. We must rescue the Ringelblum Archive!" When the first cache was found in 1946, she helped organize its contents.

In early postwar Poland, Rachel was an active member of the Central Jewish Historical Commission in Lodz and the Jewish Historical Institute in Warsaw. She began collecting and editing testimonies from survivors for both institutions. She prepared a questionnaire and a guide for taking oral testimony. In November 1945, she participated in a fact-finding mission and inspection of the former Treblinka death camp, carried out by the Polish State Committee for the Investigation of Nazi War Crimes on Polish Soil. After this visit, she wrote a disturbing report of the mechanics of the death camp site and its victims, "In the Fields of Treblinka," published in Yiddish in 1947.

In time, Jews who favored the communist agenda of the new Soviet Poland came to control the Central Committee of Jews in Poland, and Rachel realized that there was no future for Holocaust research—or for her—in Poland. In 1950, she made the difficult decision to leave the land of her birth—and the lost Jewish Polish intellectual landscape she had known so well—and to immigrate to Israel.

Promoting Oral History at Yad Vashem

I neglected my literary work because I saw in this [my Holocaust writing] a mission and an obligation and a justification of the fact that I am alive.

—Rachel Auerbach

Rachel Auerbach left Poland determined to dedicate her life to chronicling the Holocaust. In Israel, Rachel devoted herself to gathering the testimonies of other survivors and to reworking her own Holocaust memoirs. She encouraged fellow refugees to tell their stories, even long after the war. She believed that recording Holocaust experiences in the first person was most important—to tell the stories as they were lived—for the sake of future generations. Beginning in March 1954, she was hired to develop and direct the Department for the Collection of Witness Testimony at Yad Vashem, the World Holocaust Remembrance Center in Israel, which had been established the previous year.

At Yad Vashem, she initiated innovative methodologies in testimony documentation, such as tape-recording interviews, a relatively new approach at the time. She encouraged survivors now living in many countries to write personal memoirs and was active in the publication of Yizkor books, memorial books focused on lost Jewish communities in Eastern Europe. At first, she was the department's only employee, but she gradually organized a staff of interviewers and catalogers, mostly fellow Eastern European survivors. She also trained several generations of archivists and researchers. By 1965, Rachel Auerbach had collected 3,000 testimonies in 15 languages.

Despite her passion for her job, it was a constant challenge for her throughout the 15 years she worked at Yad Vashem. She often disagreed with its management, all of whom were male, academically trained, professional Israeli scholars. They themselves had not experienced the war in Europe firsthand, and they viewed Holocaust research as only one part of a broader Zionist agenda—justification for the State of Israel after 2,000 years of Jewish persecution. Auerbach, on the other hand, believed the Holocaust must be viewed as a unique event of Jewish genocide.

Language was another contentious issue. Because Yad Vashem historians relied mainly on official German sources collected from the Nazis, they funded German-language documents over those in Yiddish. Rachel insisted that history be told from the Jewish, not the German, perspective—and that required Yiddish documents. Yad Vashem also promoted modern Hebrew, whereas Rachel wrote mostly in Yiddish, never gaining the same competence in written Hebrew.

In 1961, her approach to Holocaust documentation led to further conflicts. This was the year that the infamous Nazi war criminal Adolf Eichmann was tried in Israel, a significant event that captured worldwide attention. Adolf Eichmann had been the main organizer of the deportations of Jews to the death camps. Since her days working with the historian Emanuel Ringelblum, Rachel had strongly believed that the only way to understand the Holocaust was through Jewish eyewitness accounts. When she was asked by investigators to provide evidence, lists, and summaries for the trial, she insisted that the survivors' in-person statements must be at its center. At the war crime trials in Nuremburg, shortly after the war, evidence was based on documents rather than on personal testimony. She coached survivors to appear as star witnesses, along with giving her own testimony at the trial.

Even so, painful professional conflicts between Rachel and the Yad Vashem leadership continued. She was the only woman among the survivor historians, while the Yad Vashem leadership remained dominated by men. And the male leadership found her to be an opinionated female with an uncompromising vision—the annoying conscience of the Holocaust.

In 1968, when she turned 65, she was forced to retire.

Rachel Auerbach's Legacy

The memory of those who died lives in me. And also, what lives in me—the witness—is the tragedy of their doom. When I die, the others will perish with me again.

—Rachel Auerbach

Never conventional, Rachel Auerbach was no ordinary heroine of the Holocaust. She was a university-educated woman, a talented and prolific writer, an innovative psychological thinker, and a woman much ahead of her time. Before the war, Rachel was known for her sophisticated writings and publications on diverse subjects, including psychology and psychoanalysis, pedagogy, the history of literature and culture, literary criticism, modern art, and gender politics. She wrote about the plight of Jewish women in interwar Poland and about what it meant to be marginalized both as a Jew and as a woman—what feminists today refer to as "intersectionality."

After the Holocaust, the emphasis in her writing no longer specifically revolved around women's issues, though she remained an outspoken woman who never stepped back from her strong convictions. For the rest of her life, she focused on what she had witnessed during the Holocaust. For decades, with the benefit of hindsight, she reworked the material she had written in the Warsaw Ghetto and on the Aryan side of Warsaw. Her constant rewriting of her own material reflected her personal search for meaning in the Holocaust. It was her way of continually mourning what had been lost. Her final two memoirs, written in Yiddish and based on her earlier writing—*Baym Letstn Veg (On the Final Road)* and *Varshaver Tsavoes, 1933–1943 (Warsaw Testaments)*—were published toward the end of her life and after her death in 1976. Because few of her writings have been translated into English to date, the importance of her work—written before, during, and after the Holocaust—has generally been overlooked.

For her entire postwar life, Rachel Auerbach felt a deep obligation to bear witness for the Jewish people who had perished. As well as chronicling the years of death and destruction during the Holocaust, she wanted the world to remember the rich prewar life of the Jews in Poland, which she had experienced firsthand. She strongly believed that the enormity of the Nazi crimes could only be understood in relation to the world they had destroyed—a world she continued to write about. Throughout her life, she couldn't stop writing; it was her conscience at work.

Jewish Spy for the British

Vera Rosenberg Atkins

Born June 16, 1908
Died June 24, 2000

I could not abandon [the] memory [of my spies]. I decided we must find out what happened to each one.

—Vera Rosenberg Atkins

Mystery always surrounded Vera Atkins, intelligence officer for the F-Division, the France section of the British Special Operations Executive (SOE). For one thing, she was not a British citizen born in England, as most people believed. Instead, she was a Jew born in Romania—a fact that was mostly kept secret. Indeed, she was denied naturalized British citizenship until February 1944, long after she began working for the British government. But her overriding secret had to do with the nature of her work. During the Second World War, she was the headmistress of the SOE spies who parachuted into Nazi-occupied France. Few knew Vera's real role at the SOE.

The SOE was a special agency secretly launched by Prime Minister Winston Churchill after the fall of France to Nazi Germany. With its mission to build a guerilla Resistance force, especially in France, the SOE used sabotage and subversion to eventually defeat the Nazis. First hired as a secretary for the France section, Vera Atkins—brilliant, efficient, and discreet—became the informal deputy director of the F-Division and the operations officer of its SOE headquarters. Though she had neither British citizenship nor an official rank, Vera eventually controlled most of SEO's practical operations in France from her office in London. In secret documents, she was often known as "FV," F-Division Vera. She had neither the salary nor the title that reflected her critical responsibilities.

Toward the end of the war, Vera was in charge of more than 400 secret agents who were flown into Nazi-occupied France and parachuted onto land as spies for the British. She recruited potential spies, organized their training, and planned their illegal, secret entry into France. She herself was never allowed to serve behind enemy lines. Vera had too much information about the SOE stored in her encyclopedic mind, and if she were tortured by the enemy, she could reveal too much.

Within four years, from April 1941 to 1945, Vera Rosenberg Atkins became one of the most successful intelligence officers in Western Europe. Understated, smart, loyal—and often taken for granted by the men who worked with her—she was an anonymous heroine in a very male world.

A Privileged Early Life

Few who worked with her knew Vera Atkins's true background. She was born Vera Maria Rosenberg in Galatz (Galati), a port on the Danube River in Romania. She was the daughter of Maximilian Rosenberg, a German Jew from Kassel, Germany. In 1892, he had moved from Germany to Cape Town, South Africa, where he worked for a wealthy Jewish businessman. His boss, Henry Etkins, had been born in the Belorussian town of Gomel in the Pale of Settlement and fled to South Africa to escape anti-Semitic pogroms. In Cape Town, he changed his name to Atkins so that people would not know he was a Jew. Maximilian Rosenberg married Atkins's daughter, Hilda.

After starting his own business and then going bankrupt in South Africa, Max returned to Europe with his wife. The Rosenbergs and their young son temporarily settled in Romania, where Max ran a successful lumber and shipping company on the Danube River delta. It was here in Galatz that his wife gave birth to Vera, their second child and only daughter. At the time Vera was born, Galatz had a rich Jewish community of 20,000, with 18 synagogues and a yeshiva. Though Vera was not brought up to be religious, her family sometimes attended a local synagogue on Jewish holidays.

In Romania, the Rosenberg family business thrived for a while, and Max bought a stately eighteenth-century country mansion in Crasna (today Krasnoilsk), near Czernovitz, Ukraine. There had been laws preventing Jews from owning land in many parts of Eastern Europe, so Max was especially proud of owning his estate with its extensive wooded land. Here, Vera had a very privileged childhood, spending winters in the capital city of Bucharest and summers in pastoral Crasna, where she rode horses, learned to shoot, and played with her father's dogs. On holidays, the wealthy Rosenberg family often visited cosmopolitan cities like Paris and Berlin, and elegant resorts where Vera loved to ski and swim.

Because her mother had been born in England and identified as British, Vera's first language was English. Other languages, such as German, came easily to her. Vera, her mother, and her brothers were passing through Germany in 1914 on their way to a Dutch resort when the First World War, the Great War, broke out. Fearing that Max, a German national, might be called up to serve in the German army, his wife decided to stay in Cologne, Germany, with the children until the end of the war. By the time they left Germany four years later, ten-year-old Vera had learned to speak fluent German. She had also become familiar with the lifestyle and customs of the German people. With the Great War over, Vera, her mother, and her brothers returned to Romania. This international experience in Germany would serve her well when, years later, her firsthand knowledge of the German people would be an advantage in outwitting the Nazis.

Though she was a brilliant child, Vera lacked a formal education. While her two brothers were sent to upper-class prep schools in Britain, her parents insisted that she stay in Romania, where she was educated by English governesses. She later stated, "Many parents, including mine, felt a girl's education was of no particular interest or value. Girls were educated for life in general—for social life, languages, and other little essentials."

At age 15, Vera was sent to Lausanne, Switzerland, to attend finishing school. There, she learned the "social graces of a lady," aristocratic manners, proper English diction, and how to set an elegant table and prepare a perfectly made bed. She also lived in Paris for a time, attending French classes at the Sorbonne and experiencing French life. With her excellent knowledge of multiple languages, her familiarity with other cultures, and her impeccable social graces, she was considered a "well-bred" young woman of the time.

Back in Romania, the Great Depression descended on the country, and lives were radically altered. Max Rosenberg's business went bankrupt again, and he had to sell his beloved Crasna estate in 1932. He died the following year. Suddenly the Rosenberg nuclear family went from great privilege to a much lower standard of living.

While her brother was sent to Oxford University in 1931, Vera had been sent to a London secretarial school. When she returned to Romania, her father was dead. No longer financially supported by a wealthy father, Vera, now in her early 20s, had to fend for herself. She soon found a job as a secretary. Never again would she be dependent on anyone else for her livelihood. A working woman, she would make her own decisions and be independent for the rest of her life.

In her new existence in Bucharest, Vera was curious about the world around her. She led a vibrant social life. Though she was no longer wealthy, she traveled in elite circles. Because of her impressive intelligence, fluency in languages, and elegant sophistication, it was easy for her to engage with an interesting, powerful, international crowd. In the capital city of Bucharest, she made friends with Russian princes, German diplomats, and British spies. She heard the latest news about the rise of Hitler in Europe through her friend

Count von der Schulenburg, an anti-Nazi German diplomat stationed in Bucharest. She also met British upper-class businessmen, diplomats, and journalists, several of whom were undercover spies for Britain. Through these connections, she became an interpreter for an oil company for which she traveled widely and dealt with foreign clients. During her travels, she helped her British friends and colleagues obtain information about Nazi strategic planning. This would be the beginning of her covert intelligence career against Nazi Germany.

As the Nazis continued to gain power and spread their racist laws, Europe was in turmoil. When Romania formed an alliance with Nazi Germany, Vera worried that her Jewish identity would hinder her international relationships and future prospects. Never religiously observant, her response was to conceal her Jewish background. She dropped her Jewish last name, Rosenberg, and adopted her mother's maiden name, the anglicized Atkins. When the threat of a Nazi invasion became inevitable, she left Romania for good and arrived in Great Britain in 1937.

Though outwardly she appeared to be an upper-class English gentlewoman, Vera was a foreigner and a Jew. She was also the only one in her family without British citizenship. Her mother held British citizenship by birth. Her eldest brother, who had been born in the then-British colony of South Africa, had automatic British citizenship. Her younger brother had been naturalized earlier, possibly during his school days in Britain. In London with only a Romanian passport, Vera Atkins was a foreign refugee, considered by some an "enemy alien." She was, after all, a citizen of Romania, now an ally of Nazi Germany. Her father's German roots caused further suspicion. When Vera applied for British citizenship, she was refused several times. Instead, she was obliged to apply for an aliens' registration certificate.

For many years, her attempts to obtain British citizenship were rejected. Ironically, she wouldn't obtain citizenship until 1944, long after her significant intelligence work for the British government at the Special Operations Executive had begun.

In the F-Division of the British Special Operations Executive

The main purpose of the British SOE was to assist the French Resistance through espionage and sabotage after the Nazis invaded France. The SOE employed more than 13,000 people, of which 3,200 were women. Known as Churchill's Secret Army on Baker Street, the public was not told of the SOE's existence. Even Vera's mother did not know the nature of Vera's work at the time. Public recognition of its accomplishments didn't come until many years after the war.

Thanks to her former connections with British spies in Bucharest, Vera was recommended to the F-Division in February 1941 and was hired two months later. Her personal experiences living in Romania, Germany, Switzerland, France, and England equipped her with the language skills and cultural knowledge that were excellent qualifications for the job. She even had an insider's view of Hitler's rise to power thanks to her former relationships with German diplomats and British intelligence agents who had been stationed in Budapest.

Vera was hired as assistant to Colonel Maurice Buckmaster, the director of the F-Division. She soon proved her competence and loyalty to her boss and was assigned to recruit, train, and supervise the British secret agents who would be parachuted into occupied France. Her office was at 64 Baker Street in London. ("Baker Street" became a code term for the SOE.) The work inside the building was concealed from the public. Hard-working Vera often spent 18-hour days, even overnights, at Baker Street. Though she lived with her mother in Chelsea, she was rarely at home. Her mother knew only that she had "special employment" that kept her busy, day and night.

The France section of the SOE supplied secret agents and ammunition to the underground operations of the French Resistance. The secret agents Vera helped to hire came from many walks of life: a music hall drag artist, a racehorse trainer, a banker, a chef, a taxi driver, a playwright. All spoke perfect French, but they also required a deep knowledge of France for their undercover work as French-born "natives." Vera provided each agent with an alias and a convincing false identity story. She gave them fake personal items, such as letters and photos, to prove that they were French citizens. She briefed them on how to live in occupied France, giving them tips on local daily life, such as curfews, rationing, transportation information, and police regulations.

Vera interviewed her candidates in a modest room with a desk, two chairs, and a hanging lightbulb. She spoke French with them to test whether they could pass as French natives. Then, the chosen recruits were taken to unknown locations far from friends and family to learn the use of guns and explosives, followed by survival courses and parachute training. They practiced sticking to their false identities and backgrounds while being interrogated. Finally, the successful agents were parachuted into France where they met with underground reception committees. In France, they received their orders in coded personal messages, often broadcast on the BBC French Service in the evenings after the news.

Vera was not a feminist in the modern sense, but she always stood up for women and their abilities. She never let on that she had started as a secretary. As a perfect example of an ambitious woman who took on a leadership role with major responsibilities, she had a special interest in recruiting and deploying female agents as spies. Previously, women had been barred from combat roles. Instead, they were given support jobs such as typists, nurses, and drivers. Vera argued that there were certain missions that women could perform better than men. In occupied France, women were more suited to be spies because they could more easily infiltrate French society. Women were more common on the streets of France than men, most of whom had been sent to forced labor camps. Vera also argued that the German soldiers would be less suspicious of women. If a female SOE spy looked like the stereotype of a young French woman—feminine, charming, stylish—all the better. They might be treated with more respect by intrusive Nazi officials and less likely to be body-searched.

At Vera's insistence, by 1942 the British War Cabinet agreed to use women behind enemy lines as spies, secret couriers, and armed fighters. Though women were also recruited for other SOE sections, the majority were hired to be guerilla fighters in Vera's F-Division. Of the 480 SOE agents sent into France, 39 were female spies, all handpicked by Vera.

Before they were sent off to France, Vera accompanied her spies to the British airfield. There on the tarmac, she often hugged her female spies before their departure. Then she gave each of them a final security check and waved them off on their dangerous missions. After they were deployed, Vera acted as liaison to their families. This was a very sensitive task because everyone knew that those sent undercover to France might never come back.

◊◊◊

On March 24, 1944, almost three years after she was hired by the SOE, Vera was finally officially designated as F Division's intelligence officer. She remained a civilian until August, when she was given the rank of flight officer in the Women's Auxiliary Air Force (WAAF), but only after she received her British citizenship. Vera was now at the height of her career.

On June 6, 1944, the Allies crossed the Atlantic from England to capture the beaches of Normandy, France. This marked the beginning of the Nazi army's retreat from Western Europe. Vera's undercover agents were there in France to help the Allied troops. Her agents slowed down the Nazi forces newly recruited to Normandy. They cut power lines, blew up bridges and tunnels, and derailed trains carrying Nazi equipment, ammunition, and soldiers. One of Vera's female agents, Pearl Witherington, successfully led a unit of Allied soldiers against the Germans.

On May 7, 1945, Nazi Germany surrendered to the Allies. F-Division's final goal had been achieved. When it was clear that Germany had lost the war, responsibility for rebuilding France was passed on to the French Resistance leadership under General Charles de Gaulle. On January 15, 1946, the Special Operations Executive was officially dissolved, and the F-Division handed over its London headquarters to its French counterparts.

When the SOE closed, its staff was sworn to secrecy and their documents locked away or destroyed. By that summer, most SOE members had left. The staff moved back to their prior peacetime occupations or regular service in the armed forces. The public would not hear about the secret SOE for a long time.

But for Vera, the job was not over. From the F-Division, 118 of her agents were still missing. Vera believed it was her responsibility to find out what had happened to all the agents she had sent behind enemy lines. As she later expressed, "I could not abandon their memory. I decided we must find out what happened to each one." From 1945 to 1947, Vera took it upon herself to hunt down the perpetrators in Occupied Germany who had tortured and killed her agents.

Searching for Her Spies

Vera left her office on Baker Street for the last time on January 8, 1946. In her hand, she held a list of missing SOE agents. By far, most of those missing agents were from F-Division.

Vera was one of the few people interested in investigating the truth behind the missing SOE agents. Most British officials were finished with the war and did not want to look back at the difficult past. Receiving little financial assistance for her investigations from the British Foreign Office, she had to carry out her work in Occupied Germany independently. The only support she received was occasional lodging, a few foreign drivers, and, most importantly, a promotion from WAAF flight officer to squadron officer. This promotion gave her greater authority with military and diplomatic officials in Occupied Germany. When she met with Allied officials, Nazi war hunters, and the war crimes legal staff in Germany, they saw a confident, smartly dressed, formidable female squadron officer. She was, at that time, a rare woman authority figure.

To investigate what had happened to her spies—whether they were dead or alive—Vera needed to trace the circumstances under which her agents had been captured. She searched for information in Nazi documents, now in the hands of the Allies, or directly from interviews with the Nazi officials and guards who had overseen the death camps. For over a year, she investigated former concentration camps in Germany, such as Sachsenhausen, Ravensbrück, and Dachau. Many of the Nazi officials and guards she interrogated were already imprisoned for their war crimes, awaiting their own trials and executions. An exceptionally skilled interviewer with an unusually accurate memory, Vera persuaded them to tell her the truth about the fate of her agents. They also supplied her with additional information from their own dark pasts. When she interviewed Rudolf Höss, the former commander of Auschwitz, he admitted for the first time to having gassed 2,345,000 people at Auschwitz. She later gave evidence of his confessions at the Nazi war crime trials in Nuremberg. Based on her testimony, Höss was sentenced to death.

Eventually designated as a member of the British War Crimes Commission, she gathered evidence for the prosecution of other war criminals as well—for their crimes against humanity. She used the information she obtained to testify for the prosecution of Hans Kieffer, former Gestapo chief of Occupied Paris, and Johann Schwarzhuber, former overseer at Ravensbrück concentration camp. She also gathered evidence for trials at the Flossenbürg and Mauthausen concentration camps, where 24 of her male F-Division spies had been incarcerated and murdered.

But what of Vera's female spies? Several of the women from F-Division had been captured by the Nazis and sent as prisoners to concentration camps in Germany and Poland before they disappeared. It was difficult to find more information about their fates—whether they were murdered or just currently missing. After the war, women spies were especially vulnerable. Considered civilians rather than prisoners of war, they lacked the military status that would allow them to return to England more quickly. It was therefore hard to trace the female SOE agents who were still alive.

Her search led her to Ravensbrück, the infamous women's concentration camp in Germany, where thousands of women—many of them French—had died of hunger, hanging, gassing, shooting, or medical experimentation. When the Russian Red Army liberated the camp in 1945, only a small percentage of imprisoned women had survived. Vera found out that among those who had been murdered in Ravensbrück were three of her agents: Violette Szabo, Lilian Rolfe, and Denise Bloch. In March 1946, she interviewed the camp overseer of Ravensbrück, whose information led her to find that four more of her spies—Vera Leigh, Diana Rowden, Andrée Borrel, and Nora Inayat Khan—had been taken from Ravensbrück and sent to be murdered in the Natzweiler death camp in Alsace, France. In November 1946, Vera was asked to join the prosecution team for the Ravensbrück criminal trial to indict the Nazi murderers.

In the end, Vera established the fate of almost all of her 118 missing spies—where, when, and how they were killed. Of her 39 female agents, 16 were murdered by the Nazis.

After the War

When Vera returned to London from Germany, she was unemployed and needed a job. Her skills and hard work as an intelligence officer and as a witness to the prosecution of Nazi criminals were no longer needed. Instead, she was hired as office manager for a division of UNESCO (United Nations Educational, Scientific and Cultural Organization), at the Central Bureau for Educational Visits and Exchanges. This organization promoted international cooperation and arranged student exchanges around the world. With her well-honed management skills, she soon became the division's director.

Vera Rosenberg Atkins never married and had no children. Instead, she dedicated her life to keeping alive the memory of the Second World War Resistance movement. Vera defended her decision to send women behind enemy lines, pointing out that they had been exceptionally brave and given away no intelligence information, even when they were about to be executed. She wanted the Special Operations Executive and its agents, both dead and alive, to be remembered for their valiant work in defeating the Nazis. She initiated and promoted postwar lecture tours for the surviving agents. She organized memorials, wrote promotional pieces, and gave interviews to authors and screen writers interested in the war years and the SOE. Her sharp memory benefited many writers and historians who wrote about the Second World War. Though Vera never wrote her own story of her time as head of a spy network, the SOE was no longer a secret. Thanks to her generous insights, several books, television productions, and films about the SOE and its agents were eventually produced.

In 1948, the French government awarded Vera Atkins the Croix de Guerre for her work in France. In 1995, it paid its highest tribute to her as *Commandeur de la Légion d'honneur* (Commander of the Legion of Honor). But Vera received no recognition from Great Britain until 1997—over a half century after the war had ended—when she was finally honored as a Commander of the Order of the British Empire.

Why did it take so long for Vera to be recognized as a heroine in Britain? Anti-Semitism and misogyny probably played roles. She continued to be a controversial figure—a formidable and unusual woman—born in what had now become a communist country. It was the beginning of the Cold War, and there were those who suspected she was a communist sympathizer aligned with the Soviet Union because of humanitarian remarks she had made in public. Criticism of her decision to send women into combat zones continued. When it was later discovered that SOE radios had been captured by the Nazis, conspiracy theories against the secretive SOE were ramped up, and Vera was blamed. In addition, as a self-sufficient woman who had never married, her sexual orientation was always under scrutiny.

In her later years, Vera remained absorbed with SOE affairs. She led a busy social life, partying more in her 70s and 80s than she ever had, even in her youthful days in Bucharest. She made sure she was never alone and invited many old friends and acquaintances to dinner, to tea, and for drinks. She eventually settled in Winchelsea, Sussex, in a cottage left to her by an aunt. On a clear day, she could see France from her window.

Vera Rosenberg Atkins died in Hastings, Sussex, at the age of 92. To the end of her life, Vera defended her decision to send female spies behind enemy lines. She and her agents had helped bring about the defeat of the Nazis in France, and her work after the war played a significant role in bringing some powerful Nazi perpetrators to justice. Vera showed that women were as capable as men of fighting a war against hate.

Surrogate Mother of Many

Lena Kuchler
Silberman

Born 1910 (or January 28, 1912)
Died August 6, 1987

[The woman] unfolded the dirty scrap of paper and read aloud: Mira (Miriam) Mosner. Born August 20, 1941, in Lvov. The names of the parents were not given. August 20, 1941? That was the date of my own daughter's birth! And she, too, had been born in Lvov and been called Miriam.... It all matched! Age, sex, place of birth—except for one detail that did not match. My own little Miriam was dead.... We had seen her die.

—Lena Kuchler Silberman

This was all that Lena would say about her own infant daughter who had died of malnourishment during the worst of times for Jews in Lvov, Poland (today Lviv, Ukraine). Though she never mentioned the exact date or place of her baby's death, it is known that her child—not yet one year old—had died in the early days of the brutal Nazi occupation of Poland, when Lena and her then-husband were themselves struggling to stay alive. Three months after Miriam's birth, in November 1941, the Nazis set up the ghetto in Lvov. Many children died in ghettos from starvation, disease, and lack of adequate clothing and shelter during the cold winter months. By March 1942, the Nazis deported Jews from the Lvov ghetto to Belzec, the death camp where almost half a million Jews were murdered.

Baby Miriam may have died of starvation inside the ghetto. Or she may have died while her parents were in hiding from ghetto deportations. In either case, Miriam's parents were desperate and probably destitute at the time. It is not surprising that they could not meet the needs of their tiny infant or keep her alive.

Lena Kuchler never got over the grief of losing her child. To soften this grief and lessen her guilt, she made it her mission to keep other Jewish children alive. Disguised as a Christian Pole, she smuggled Jewish children out of the Warsaw Ghetto into Catholic institutions and Christian Polish homes in the countryside. After the war, she became a member of the Jewish Committee in Krakow, Poland, and established a home for displaced Jewish orphans in Zakopane, a resort in the Tatra Mountains. When anti-Semitism in the town became intolerable and dangerous, she took her 100 children, ages 3 to 15, to France, illegally crossing dangerous borders as they traveled from Poland through Czechoslovakia.

By September 1946, she and the children entered France to await legal immigration into Palestine. In late 1948, she and her charges—most of whom had been with her since their wretched post-war days in Krakow in 1945—sailed from France to the newly founded State of Israel. In total, she helped rehabilitate the lives of about 170 Jewish refugee orphans and rescued them from poverty, illness, and trauma.

Lena Kuchler Silberman's lifework followed in the footsteps of Dr. Janusz Korczak, the heroic Jewish Polish educator and orphanage director in the Warsaw Ghetto, who accompanied his Jewish orphans on the train to the gas chambers. One major difference is that, while Korczak and his orphans were murdered, Lena Kuchler and her orphans survived the Holocaust, and she was able to offer her children a future. Another major difference is that Dr. Korczak's story is well known, while few have heard of Lena Kuchler Silberman, except perhaps in Israel. It is time for Lena's story to be more widely told.

Early Life

Lena Kuchler was born in 1910 (or maybe, as her forged Aryan document stated, January 28, 1912) and grew up in Wieliczka, Poland, 16 kilometers (10 miles) southeast of the urban center of Krakow. Her parents were Sara (Brenner) and Eliyahu Kuchler, observant Jews of little financial means. Her father probably studied Hebrew texts all day, as was traditional in Orthodox households. Her mother ran a store while caring for the children and her husband. They lived in a modest house with two bedrooms in the attic. As the eldest child, Lena was lucky to share one of the two attic bedrooms with her parents and her grandmother, while the other six children slept together in the next bedroom.

Though her family was poor, Lena was smart, ambitious, and determined to get a good education. Fortunately, the family lived close to Krakow, where she could attend a Hebrew academic high school. Later, she went to the Jagiellonian University in Krakow, where she majored in child psychology and education—both subjects that would become useful for her future calling. For a time before the war, she was a teacher in a Jewish school and taught in a teacher training seminary.

When her mother died in 1939 and Poland was invaded by the Nazis, her brothers fled east to Siberia in the Soviet Union. Now married, she and her husband moved to Lvov, then Poland (today Lviv, Ukraine) where, two years later, their daughter, Miriam, was born. Their baby's death devastated Lena, but her husband declared they would have a better chance to survive without responsibility for a child. Trying to pass as Aryans would be difficult enough for just the two of them. They fled to Aryan Warsaw to blend in with the larger urban masses. By then, their relationship was strained and they lived apart. Her husband disappeared with a German woman, hoping to save his own life, which he did. He left Lena when she needed him the most.

Now alone, Lena bleached her hair blond and moved in with a Christian family outside the ghetto walls under an assumed identity—Leontena Zofia Relicz from Buczacz. No one was aware that she was a Jew. At first, she worked in a German factory but eventually became a bookkeeper for a German company. She sometimes took life-threatening chances by sneaking into the Warsaw Ghetto to smuggle out Jewish children. She helped place these children in a Catholic convent that served as an orphanage. Always persuasive, Lena talked the reluctant presiding priest into accepting several Jewish children.

Fearing for her life after several close calls with the Gestapo on the streets of Warsaw, she found a job far away from the city. She became a governess for a family of Polish nobility on an estate in a remote farming community called Olchowek, located not far from Treblinka. She cared for baby Gigi and four-year-old Krysia while their parents, Count Ludwig Niedzelsky and his wife, Irene, traveled back and forth from Warsaw. Lena and the children soon became very attached to each other.

During her time in Olchowek, no one suspected her of being a Jew. One day on their estate, she found a sick, elderly, starving Jew hiding in a ditch. He had escaped from the death camp at Treblinka. She helped him move to a safer spot and brought him food—until one day he was discovered and shot. This was a reminder for Lena of her own vulnerability as an undercover Jew.

When the Soviet Russians defeated the Nazis and liberated Olchowek in 1944, they confiscated the wealth and property of her employers. The Soviets saw peasants as victims and landowners as wealthy exploiters. The Soviet soldiers took over the Niedzelsky family's estate and house, leaving only one room for the entire family, including Lena.

With her power of persuasion, Lena talked the victorious Soviets into allowing her to open a school on the estate for the illiterate children of the village. Knowing the communist preference for the working and lower classes, she emphasized that she was a servant in the Niedzelsky household and that, as a former teacher, she wanted to help the illiterate peasant community. Lena's school started with 10 children of all ages and soon grew to 30, including her own two wards, Gigi and Krysia. All the children loved her and soon learned to read and write. She loved them right back.

With "liberation" from the Nazis by the Soviets, the times had changed and many roles were reversed. Her former employers, once wealthy, now depended on Lena and her teacher's salary. For the next half year, she stayed loyal to her former employers, until she realized it was time to move on. She was ready to reconnect with her Jewish identity. Though she may not have recognized it then, there were more children for her to care for—this time Jewish refugee children.

The Surviving Jewish Children

How could I expect them to be literate when they [the Jewish refugee children] had spent so many [of their] precious [learning] years hiding in forests, in cellars, in attics?

—Lena Kuchler Silberman

Hiding from her roots, her Jewish identity, and her own people, Lena had spent almost two years in the countryside taking care of Christian people's children. She may have been unaware, or in denial, of the surviving Jewish children who had experienced horrible atrocities in the war and now faced uncertain futures.

The Nazis had a despicable reputation for killing young children. In German institutions alone, 5,000 to 7,000 German children with physical and mental disabilities were murdered. Nazi Germany and its collaborators killed about 1.5 million Jewish children and tens of thousands of Romani children. Because they provided forced labor to the Nazis, able Jewish adolescents, ages 13 to 18, had greater chances for survival. But infants and younger children were unproductive and considered "useless eaters." German authorities often selected the little ones—along with the elderly, the ill, and the disabled—as the first victims in the death camps.

Some children found ways to stay alive. Because they were agile, they could scramble under ghetto walls and smuggle much needed food, medicines, and supplies from the outside. Older children, some as young as 13 or 14, joined various forms of underground Resistance and armed Jewish youth groups that fought the Nazis. Others fled to parts of the Soviet Union still unoccupied by the Nazis. Many children escaped to the woods where they lived in family camps in the forest. And some were hidden with Christian families or in convents, churches, and orphanages.

After the Allies defeated the Nazis in 1945, Jewish survivors began the painful search for remaining family members. Local Jewish committees in Europe and international refugee organizations tried to register and trace the living and account for the dead. Parents searched for the children they had left with Christian families or in Catholic institutions.

Some young children did not even know their own last names or where and when they were born. They had little or no memory of their real parents nor knowledge of their Jewish origins. The only parents and family that they knew were their Christian rescuers. For many, it was a shock to discover their Jewish identity. Consequently, when parents, relatives, or Jewish organizations went to retrieve them, the children were resistant to leave behind the only people they knew.

Most surviving teenagers were orphans. Not only had they been traumatized by their experiences but they were often homeless. With no adult guidance, they had to recover alone from past traumas—their forced separation from parents, their experience as prisoners in concentration camps, or their rugged life as fighters with the partisans. Many were malnourished and ill. And the Jewish communal organizations that were supposed to provide shelter for them were overextended, underfunded, understaffed, and unable to properly care for orphaned children. It would become Lena Kuchler's purpose to shelter and defend some of these Jewish orphans.

Lena after Liberation

*After the war I was broken and crushed, with nothing
to live for. The children saved me—by helping them, I
redeemed myself.*

—Lena Kuchler Silberman

After the war, Lena's own salvation was centered on saving Jewish
children. This became her purpose for living. After leaving
Olchowek, Lena returned to the place of her birth to search for
remaining family members. In her hometown, she recognized no
one. When she entered her parents' old house, the Pole living there
rebuked her for returning and physically assaulted her.

She then went to Warsaw to search for news of her beloved sister Fela, who had been a partisan fighter outside Warsaw. They had
briefly met the year before, while Warsaw was still in Nazi hands.
When she found out that Fela had been tortured to death by the
Nazis just days before liberation, Lena grieved and questioned her
own existence. Why had *she* been left alive? What was the purpose
of her survival?

In despair and running a fever, Lena took a train to the
Krakow station, where her cousin Frania found her, ill and dis-
oriented. Her cousin was now a high-ranking communist official
who went by the name of Lieutenant-Colonel Franciska Eliaszowna
Honig of the Polish Army. Frania took Lena to her comfortable
apartment in Krakow and nursed her back to health. She invited
Lena to stay with her. For the first time in a long time, Lena was
able to enjoy the luxuries of Frania's books and paintings, and to
play Chopin's music on the piano.

When she felt better, Lena returned to the Jagiellonian
University, where she reconnected with her old professor who had
been imprisoned as a Polish intellectual at Dachau concentration
camp. Back in his old job at the university, he hired Lena to do
research for his forthcoming encyclopedia of psychology and en-

couraged her to continue her studies now that the war was over.

Still, Lena questioned what to do with the rest of her life. Did she really want a career as an academic, one step further away from the children she loved to teach? Could she continue to hide away from her own traumas—the death of her daughter, the separation from her husband, and the feelings of guilt that so many people had died while she had managed to survive by hiding her Jewish identity? She wanted to further her education, but she soon discovered that with her bold voice she could accomplish more important things.

Commitment to the Future

One day, Lena wandered into the Krakow Jewish Committee headquarters on Dluga Street, where survivors went for help. She saw haggard, hungry Jewish refugees, some still wearing the striped uniforms of the concentration camps, waiting to receive clothing and food. Always the teacher, she asked where the children could be found. She was told to go to the second floor of the building.

What she saw there was appalling. In a filthy, barren room, more than 50 malnourished Jewish children—sick in body and mind—were living under conditions that tore at her heart. Some were as young as two or three; others were teenagers. Many had been liberated from concentration camps. Others had been dropped off by priests and farmers who had sheltered them during the war but would or could no longer provide for them. All were hungry, dirty, ragged, and shoeless.

Moved by the sight of these abandoned children, Lena left and returned to Dluga Street that same day with four loaves of bread. She cut them into small pieces and smeared them with butter and jam. The children could hardly believe their eyes! They grabbed at the morsels and begged for more. The next day, she returned with more food. She visited the children at Dluga Street again and again, bringing food, clothing, blankets, and medicine.

Slowly, the children began to trust her. She washed and scrubbed their frail bodies, which were often covered in sores, boils, and scars. She massaged their skeletal limbs, some with broken bones that had not properly healed. The emotional connection between Lena and the children became stronger with each passing day. Some even began to call her "mother." And they in turn became "her children." Her future purpose was now obvious: to restore these children to physical, emotional, and psychological health.

Always a determined woman, Lena sought out those officials who could equip her with funding and supplies for her children. Cutting ahead of a long line, she burst boldly into the office of the person in charge of food supplies and convinced him to give her 2,000 kilograms (4,400 pounds) of sugar, which she then traded for flour, oil, shoes, and clothing. Supported by her high-ranking cousin Frania, she continued to receive more food, clothing, and supplies from local agencies.

To further her goals, Lena became a member of the Krakow Jewish Committee. She worked with the Committee to find a permanent shelter for the orphans, away from the substandard life at Dluga Street. She sought a place that could offer healthier living conditions—a combined children's home, school, and sanatorium away from the city. The Committee found a large, old house on an estate in Zakopane, a winter health resort high in the Tatra Mountains. The fresh mountain air would help bring the sick children back to health. Lena brought 60 of her Jewish orphans to Zakopane. Here, the physically and emotionally ill children could recuperate far away from the turmoil they had experienced in their short lives.

Her next task was to find caregivers—doctors, nurses, teachers, counselors. Lena hired young Jewish women who had lost their own families, some of them former prisoners in nearby Auschwitz. She told them, "These children are our orphans and we must become surrogate mothers to them all. Since you do not have children of your own, you must find the energy and love to take these children into your hearts." Though they worked for little or no salary, her staff became fully committed to the children, as she was. Together, they gave the children what they needed: protection, shelter, food, clothing, medicine—and, most important, a sense of family.

The Mixed Blessings of Zakopane

The latest events in Zakopane reinforced my realization that the children's fate is intrinsically connected to the fate of Jews in Poland.

—Lena Kuchler Silberman

Lena and her children arrived in Zakopane in the summer of 1945. Besides being the director and their Hebrew teacher, Lena interacted closely with the children on a daily basis. She personally nurtured them—for their sake and for her own. Just as she and the caregivers had bonded with the children, the orphans became like brothers and sisters. While there had been in-fighting between the children on Dluga Street, now the teenagers began to look out for the little ones. The older girls from the convents, who still practiced their Catholic rituals, were now accepted by the tough older boys who initially had been very hostile to them. Children with disabilities were helped by those without. Sounds of laughter soon echoed throughout the children's home in Zakopane.

The number of children in the home was fluid, with new children arriving often and others leaving. Twenty new orphans came from Warsaw and Lodz, sick and hungry. Lena took them all in. She found five ailing Jewish children in a remote and poor Christian orphanage. Twelve teenagers from Zakopane left for the Labor Zionist group near Lodz where they were to be illegally smuggled into Palestine, which was still under British mandate. When their emigration failed, they returned to Lena. Other children were eventually found by their biological parents and taken out of Zakopane. When another Jewish orphanage was closed after several anti-Semitic attacks, 30 additional children were taken to Zakopane.

But the peaceful atmosphere at the Zakopane children's home did not last for very long. In September 1945, the older children were sent to the local school where they were taunted and attacked for being Jewish. Then came more serious attacks on the streets by individuals and members of the White Polish Brigades, a band of anti-Semitic vigilantes. Afraid to leave the safety of their home in the face of such events, the Jewish children and staff became isolated on their estate grounds.

Lena had known that Zakopane had a reputation for being anti-Semitic, but she had hoped that their estate was sufficiently secluded and they would not be harmed. Then came an especially threatening attack on their Zakopane home, which sent Lena to seek protection from the Jewish Committee in Krakow and the Central Jewish Committee in Warsaw. Showing little concern for the children, the leaders of the Jewish committees, under the influence of the Soviet regime by this time, told her to remain with the children for the sake of a "democratic" Poland. Instead of protecting the children, they offered her weapons to fight off the attackers. When the next anti-Semitic attack occurred, it was Lena's teenage boys and girls who took up the weapons and chased the intruders away. Many of the teenagers had training and experience with guns and explosives from their days in the partisans and underground Resistance.

Between the anti-Semitic attacks and the rise of the communist political agenda in Soviet Poland, Lena recognized it was time to leave. The children already carried terrible memories of their losses and devastation in Poland. Lena knew that to further heal the children's physical and emotional trauma, they must emigrate from Poland.

The children's home in Zakopane had been operating for a year by then. Its greatest success was that the bond between Lena, the staff, and the children had grown ever stronger since Dluga Street. But would this bond be strong enough for the children to follow her out of Poland? Lena first addressed the issue of the children who had surviving family members in Poland. Sixteen children would need to be picked up by their relatives. Then, she gave the older children a choice of whether to leave or not. One 13-year-old boy was reluctant to emigrate because his sister, his only surviving relative, was still living in a convent. Lena gave him travel money to reach his sister and invite her to join them, which they both did. In the end, Lena asked all the children, age nine and older, whether they were prepared to leave Poland with her. To the last one, they all agreed.

The Long Journey

They left Zakopane on March 14, 1946, at four o'clock in the morning. Children and caretakers crowded into a huge open truck, covered with a tarpaulin so that no one would suspect what was going on. Lena had not informed the Krakow Jewish Committee or the Warsaw Central Jewish Committee of their departure. She was afraid they might prevent their move. She later wrote to the Krakow Jewish Committee: "I did not see any option for [the children] staying in Zakopane or any other place [in Poland]. I think that, after the hell they went through, I cannot expose them to these dangers in the name of building a new [Soviet] democracy."

Instead, she accepted an offer from a secret relief organization, Vaad Hatzalah, which promised them passage through the strictly guarded border crossings and continued support in France. This organization also provided passports for most of the children. Finding themselves four passports short, four little ones were smuggled into backpacks carried by Lena and some teenagers. When one of the little children relieved himself inside the backpack, they laughed it off to the guards at a border crossing as a leaking water bottle.

By September 1946, Lena had brought 100 children into France, where they waited to immigrate to Palestine. During their temporary stay there, she ran a home for her displaced Jewish orphans in Bellevue, just outside Paris. She became director of this new children's home funded by French and American Jewish charities. The Joint, the global Jewish humanitarian organization based in the United States, supplied her with food, clothing, and upkeep of the home.

While they were in France, the children planned a surprise Mother's Day celebration for Lena. They organized and decorated the dining hall and put up a poster with a large photo of Lena and giant letters spelling "KUCHLER." The younger children led Lena from her room to the dining area. As Lena passed through the halls, the children threw flower petals that they had collected. One older boy wrote and read aloud: "Today is dedicated to our mother. We were not supposed to celebrate this day, since our mothers were killed. But we are celebrating.... Because we have a mother who is devoted to us and loves us.... We appreciate her toil, sacrifice, and care. We appreciate that she saved our lives."

"Mother" and Children in Israel

Lena was not an active Zionist, and her original plan after the war was to stay in Poland. Yet after she and her children experienced the bleak reality of anti-Semitic postwar Poland, she believed they would be safest in the new Jewish state. At the time, which other country was willing to give visas to 100 Jewish orphaned refugee children?

In late 1948, Lena and her charges sailed from Marseille, France, to Haifa, Israel. The children were taken to Kibbutz Schiller, where they were legally adopted by members of the *kibbutz*. Lena relocated to Tel Aviv, where she studied psychology in a seminary for kindergarten and school teachers, worked as an educational superintendent, and set up an educational psychology service center in Givatayim for kindergartens and schools. A street in Tel Aviv is named after her, and there is a plaque commemorating her achievements in Givatayim. She retired from her work as an educator in 1972.

Using her strong voice again, Lena Kuchler Silberman wrote one of the first books specifically about women and children who had experienced the Holocaust. Her memoir, *Mayne Kinder* (My Children), in Yiddish, was published in Paris, as early as 1948. The Hebrew version of her book, *My Hundred Children*, was published in 1959 by Yad Vashem and became required reading in Israeli schools.

In 1957, at age 47, Lena Kuchler Silberman gave birth to a baby girl, whom she and her husband, Mordecai Silberman, named Shira. As she herself stated, her new daughter became her 101st living child. Lena never lost contact with her many other children. They came to visit her for holidays and special occasions. A loving and gifted educator, Lena Kuchler Silberman remained the surrogate mother of her "100 children"—and their heroine!

One Righteous Woman

Irena Gut (Gutowna) Opdyke

Born May 5, 1922
Died May 17, 2003

The war was a series of choices made by many people. Some of those choices were as wicked and shameful to humanity as anything in history. But some of us made other choices. I made mine.

—Irena Gut Opdyke

In the summer of 1954, Irena Gut, a Christian Polish woman in her early thirties, visits a chicken farm in rural Connecticut as an overnight guest of Jewish Polish Holocaust survivors. The Jewish immigrants had bought a 16-hectare (40-acre) farm after they arrived from Europe in 1951, resettled with the help of HIAS, the American Jewish refugee organization. The land has marshes filled with red-winged blackbirds weaving between bulrushes and fields of wild daisies. The survivors have a seven-year-old daughter with curly dark hair, a freckled nose, and bright hazel eyes. She loves it when Irena comes to visit the farm because Irena pays attention to her. The little girl with the dark curls is the only child of older parents who are busy feeding 5,000 chickens, and collecting, grading, and selling eggs from the chicken coops. Because they live in the country and other houses are far from their farm, there are no neighborhood kids to play with.

When she comes to visit, Irena takes the girl by the hand and together they walk through the fields and pick dozens of daisies, which they bring back to the house in a wicker basket. For hours, they talk between themselves and braid daisies into crowns that they place high on top of their heads, pretending to be princesses. Even though one is a child and the other an adult, they are good friends.

How did Irena come to visit the chicken farm? One day, on a crowded beach in Coney Island—in Brooklyn, New York, where she lived and worked in a garment factory—Irena overheard a woman sitting on a nearby blanket speaking Polish. Happy to hear her native language, Irena introduced herself. On their blankets in the sand, she and the other woman, Ruth, discovered that they were both immigrants, refugees from Poland, who had arrived in the United States in 1949.

They shared common histories and talked about their lives during the Holocaust years. Irena, a Christian Pole, had worked as a housekeeper for a Nazi army major in Tarnopol, Poland. She rescued 16 Jews by hiding them right under her employer's nose, in the cellar of his villa. Ruth survived the war years in Aryan Warsaw, undercover as a Christian Pole while working with the Jewish underground Resistance. Both had displayed enormous courage during dangerous times.

After their meeting, Irena and Ruth became fast friends, and in the coming years they spent many hours together. Ruth, a fashion designer and seamstress in Manhattan, hired Irena to work with her in her tailoring shop. During the hot New York summers, Irena often joined Ruth when she visited her sister's farm in the country.

On the farm as they gather daisies together, the little Jewish girl, daughter of Holocaust survivors, does not know that her grownup friend Irena was once a smuggler, a spy, and a heroine in her former life—never a princess. She does not know about Irena's past heroic deeds of hiding fugitive Polish Jews—like the little girl's parents had been—and smuggling them to safety.

For a long time, Irena did not talk about her past. During the Second World War in Poland—knowing full well that Poles aiding Jews risked the death penalty—Irena, then a young Polish nursing student barely out of her teens, made some dangerous decisions. Decades later, Irena Gut Opdyke received the Righteous

Among the Nations Award from Yad Vashem, the World Holocaust Remembrance Center in Israel, honoring non-Jews who endangered their own lives to save Jews during the Holocaust.

Beginnings

The same Irena Gut (in Polish, the feminine Gutowna) was born in 1922 in Kozienice, a small village in eastern Poland. She was the eldest of five daughters born to Maria (Rebies) and Wladyslaw Gut. When she was just a baby, Irena was saved by a dog who tugged at her diaper to keep her from falling into the river near their house while no one was watching. From that day forward, her parents, religious Catholics, always believed she was meant to do great things in her life.

Irena spent her early teen years with her family in Upper Silesia, six kilometers (four miles) from the German border. Though her parents were patriotic Poles, many of her neighbors were of German descent, *Volksdeutsche*, and so she learned to speak German in school and on the streets. Her knowledge of the German language would be essential to her survival during the war years.

In 1939, when she was 17, Irena left her family and moved to the city of Radom to become a student at St. Mary's Hospital, one of the best nursing schools in Poland. That September, the Nazis invaded Poland, allowing Soviet Russia, ally of Nazi Germany at that time, to invade eastern parts of then Poland according to their Nazi-Soviet Non-Aggression Pact. In the face of that danger, her parents begged Irena to come home, but she decided to stay at the hospital to nurse the wounded.

Later, Irena became part of a Polish medical team sent eastward by Red Cross trucks and trains to help the retreating Polish soldiers. As the Soviet Russian army advanced, she found herself part of a beleaguered, starving Polish medical unit—enemy of the Soviets—hidden in the woods near the Soviet border. She was by far the youngest member of the group.

One day, she was left alone on the outskirts of a town to mark the trail, while the others looked for food. She was spotted by a gang of Soviet soldiers. Defenseless, she was attacked, raped, and left unconscious. Other kinder Russian soldiers found her and brought her to a Soviet hospital.

When Irena regained consciousness, she found herself in a hospital in Tarnopol (today Ternopil, Ukraine), a Polish captive of the Soviet Russians who controlled the area. Though she was a prisoner, because of her nursing skills she was allowed to care for patients in the short-staffed hospital. When her superior, a Russian medical administrator, made unwanted sexual advances toward her, she fled. She escaped eastward to the small village of Svetlana, where she connected with a female doctor who gave her refuge. In gratitude, she became the doctor's assistant and roomed with her for a year. When the Germans and the Soviets made an agreement that temporarily allowed Poles to return to their families, Irena left in search of hers.

Polish Prisoner in Nazi Radom

I did not become a resistance fighter, a smuggler of Jews, a defier of...the Nazis all at once. One's first steps are always small: I [began] by hiding food under a fence.

—Irena Gut Opdyke

Irena found her family in Nazi-occupied Radom, but by this time conditions had worsened for all Poles. Surrounded, first by hostile Soviets, then by racist Nazis, the Polish population suffered greatly during the Second World War. Polish intellectuals and professionals were fired from their jobs. Irena's father, an architect and a chemist by training, was now sewing slippers to help support the family. He was later sent to a nearby town as a forced laborer to supervise the ceramics factory that he had designed years before.

Insisting on their own racial supremacy, the Nazis considered the Polish people inferior, just a step above the Jews. Like the Jews,

Poles were considered *Untermenschen*, sub-humans. Eventually, many Poles would be forced to wear armbands with a "P"—like the Star of David armbands that Jews were forced to wear—distinguishing them from the local Germans. Polish military and political leaders were sent to concentration camps, while the Nazis forced young and able Poles into labor to help their war effort, often transporting them to Germany. Many Polish residents of Radom went hungry because they received much smaller food rations than the German *Volksdeutsche*.

Now 18 years old, Irena managed to obtain working papers. But before she could find a job, she was caught outside a church in a Nazi roundup of Polish civilians. She was forced into labor and separated from her family. She slept in crowded barracks at night and worked in a munitions factory during the day, packing ammunition into boxes for no wages. One day, hungry and anemic, she fainted on the job at the feet of a Nazi major.

When she recovered, Irena was brought to the office of Nazi *Wehrmacht* Major Eduard Rügemer. The older Nazi officer took an interest in her because she was young, blond, blue-eyed, and beautiful. She also had a German-sounding last name, Gut, and spoke German very well. He transferred her to work in a soldiers' mess hall at a local hotel that catered to German officials and soldiers. There, she was assigned to work as a waitress and to translate Polish into German for her boss, the Nazi commanding officer. Most important for Irena was that her boss was in charge of food. Irena served the Nazi officers three meals a day: roast chicken, pork chops, knockwurst, sauerkraut, beet soup, chocolate cakes. After the officers finished their meals, she was allowed to leave with the leftovers. Irena now had all the food she needed and often shared it with others.

Before the Nazi invasion of 1939, Poland had the highest population of Jews in all of Europe, 3 million out of a total population of 33 million. This was one reason that the Nazis designated Poland as the center for Jewish destruction. Jews from all over Europe were sent to Poland to be murdered in ghettos and concentration camps.

In Radom, approximately 30,000 Jews, one-quarter of the city's population, were forced into two ghettos, one in central Radom, the other in the suburb of Glinice. The Glinice ghetto was surrounded by a long fence of tall wooden poles and barbed wire. At the only entrance was a sign: Danger of contamination. Do not enter.

From certain places in the hotel, Irena could see the poverty and death that was taking place behind the barbed-wire fence of the ghetto. Grateful that she was relatively safe and no longer hungry, her compassion grew for those who were less fortunate—the Jews. She often walked outside the barbed fence of the Jewish ghetto. One day, she made a decision: She bore a hole under the fence and left a basket filled with food. The next morning, the basket was empty. With her own easy access to food, Irena left a food basket under the fence each day.

Meanwhile, every day the Nazi loudspeaker in Radom blasted its message: "Whoever helps a Jew will be punished by death." Irena had never planned to be a rescuer of Jews, but smuggling food into the ghetto became the first step in her bold rescue missions.

Rescuing Jews in Tarnopol

By spring 1942, the war had accelerated, and the Nazis advanced eastward, farther into the Soviet Union, enemy of Nazi Germany since June 22, 1941. The Radom munitions factory where Irena worked was now relocated to Tarnopol, closer to the fighting. In Tarnopol, the three-block facility escalated its production of weapons, where they could more easily be delivered to the Nazi army at the frontline of the fighting. In the Tarnopol factory compound, a four-story hotel was converted into a dining hall and living quarters for the Nazi officers in charge.

Transferred to the compound in Tarnopol, a city she already knew, Irena continued to work as a waitress. Serving high-ranking Nazi officials in the dining hall, Irena could easily overhear their strategic plans. It was a perfect position from which to spy on the Nazis.

Along with her job as a waitress, Irena was placed in charge of the laundry room, where Jewish workers were forced to wash and mend Nazi uniforms. She supervised 12 workers from the nearby forced labor camp—deported Jewish women and men formerly from Germany—trucked into the munitions compound daily. Most of the Jewish laundry workers in her charge had been educated and wealthy before the war. They included a medical student, a lawyer, a nurse, a businessman, and a dressmaker. Working together each day, she befriended them and treated them with kindness and compassion. She gave them food, which she hid in laundry baskets. She also informed them of any Nazi plans she overheard in the dining room that could affect them as Jews.

In the dining hall, she waited on *Wehrmacht* Major Rügemer and his high-ranking friend, the local head of the SS (*Schutzstaffel*), whose job it was to eliminate all Jews from that part of Poland. Whenever she served his table, the major was always friendly toward her. At one point, she asked him whether she could have extra help for the laundry, and he agreed to let her choose more Jewish women from the labor camp. Whenever she overheard the Nazi officials sharing plans for a new raid on the work camp or the ghetto, she warned her friends. If they knew about a roundup ahead of time, some might be able to flee into the forest. By August 1942, the deportation of Jews from Tarnopol to the Belzec death camp had begun.

In the spring of 1943, the Nazis began to speed up the deportation of the remaining Jews in Tarnopol to the death camps. Several of Irena's laundry workers decided that it would be safer to hide in the surrounding woods, and they asked Irena for help. Trading vodka and cigarettes stolen from the supply room, she borrowed a horse and cart from a nearby farmer to transport four Jewish refugees. She hid them on the floor of the horse-drawn carriage under bags of potatoes and hay. The following week, she returned to the pine forest with two more Jewish fugitives. She promised to return with food as often as she could. Irena, now 21 years of age, had become a smuggler of six fugitive Jews.

One evening at dinner, Irena overheard the Nazis' plan to totally liquidate both the ghetto and the work camp. The final deportation of Tarnopol Jews to the Belzec death camp was coming fast, and she knew she had to help those still under her supervision in the laundry. Around the same time, the major called Irena into his office and told her he had "acquired" a villa in town. The villa had been abandoned by a wealthy Jewish architect and required some renovations to meet the major's needs. He suggested Irena supervise the renovation and become his private housekeeper. At first, Irena was dismayed. She would have to quit her work at the laundry. What would happen to her remaining Jewish charges? Then she realized this was an opportunity to save them before the final deportation.

Before the major moved in, Irena checked on the villa each day. The house was large and had a cellar that could accommodate several people. The basement had been the servants' quarters with two bedrooms, a bathroom, and a kitchen. There was a coal chute on one side of the house, which led into the cellar. She also found an escape tunnel that led from behind the furnace in the cellar to a bunker beneath an outside gazebo. In moments of serious danger, there might be enough room for up to ten people to scramble into the hole for a short time. This could be a good place to hide her remaining fugitives!

Just before the Nazi soldiers searched the laundry, Irena managed to sneak her friends out of the compound and into the cellar of the villa. By then, four additional Jewish escapees had been added. Now Irena was responsible for ten hidden Jews living underneath the villa. Each day, Irena supplied them with food and water.

Once the major and Irena moved into the villa, the routine was always the same. When Major Rügemer left for the factory every morning, Irena would lock the door behind him. During the day, the fugitives would come upstairs to help her with the cleaning and the cooking. When the major returned in the evening, he would ring the doorbell. The fugitives would then quickly return to the cellar. Only after they disappeared into the basement would Irena greet her boss at the door.

Meanwhile, Irena continued to bring supplies to her other set of fugitives in the woods. She brought them food and warmer clothing for the winter. She found tarpaper to help insulate the cold dug-out bunker where they slept. When one woman in the woods became sick, Irena brought her to the cellar of the villa until she was well again. With each trip to the forest, Irena held tightly to the reins of the horse and carriage she had borrowed. Along with the horses, she held the reins of the lives of the 16 Jewish women and men she had befriended. In addition, there would soon be one more life for whom she was responsible.

One day, she was told that one of the Jewish women in hiding was pregnant. The expectant mother and her husband had agreed with the others that the baby would need to be aborted to keep everyone safe. A devout Catholic, Irena rejected this decision insisting that the baby must be born and kept alive. "Hitler will not have *this* baby!" she declared. The baby—Roman Haller, who would later in life become director of the German office of the Claims Conference representing Jewish survivors' restitution claims—was born just before the end of the war.

For eight months, the hidden refugees were kept safe inside the villa—until one day when Irena forgot to lock the door. When the major came home unexpectedly, he found two of the Jewish women in his kitchen. Rather than raging at Irena, he became silent and left. When he returned, he made a bargain with Irena. If she would agree to become his mistress, he would not disclose the secret of her hidden Jews. Reluctantly, to save her friends, Irena agreed. All that time, the major never went down into the cellar. Their bargain was kept.

There were suspicions in town that the housekeeper was the major's mistress and that Jews were hidden in the house. From the perspective of their Polish neighbors, Irena was a Polish woman working and sleeping with the Nazi enemy. In light of those rumors, Major Rügemer received orders from Berlin to fire his housekeeper.

He told Irena that her Jews must leave immediately. Meanwhile, the Nazis were losing the war, and the Soviet army, now enemy of the Nazis, was advancing toward Tarnopol. By early March 1944, the munitions factory in Tarnopol was closed and the Nazi soldiers began to withdraw.

In the midst of the Nazi exodus, Irena smuggled her Jewish fugitives out of the villa and into the forest with the others. A few days later, Major Rügemer, who was now fleeing the approaching Soviet Russians, came to take Irena westward with him to still Nazi-occupied Kielce. Now herself a fugitive, she hid on the floor of his car under a blanket for the two-day ride across Ukraine. Grateful to the major that he had never betrayed her or the fugitive Jews, she nevertheless knew she could not remain with him. No longer directly responsible for others, she needed to find her own path. She left the major the morning after they arrived and sought out Polish partisan contacts in Kielce.

Though she had already lived through extraordinary circumstances for a young woman of her age, Irena had never before had a meaningful intimate relationship. While she was considering joining the partisans in Kielce, Irena fell in love with her partisan contact, a handsome guerilla fighter. Following her lover, she lived deep in the forest just outside Kielce and became a courier for the local Polish partisans. She was about to marry her lover when he was killed in an ambush.

After his death, she felt she had little to lose and fearlessly continued delivering packets of money and messages to other Polish partisans, often by bicycle, until the war was over. By spring 1945, Irena, finally able to rest, fell ill with pneumonia brought on by exhaustion. She was only 23 years old and had lived through what seemed like a lifetime of perilous events.

After the Holocaust in Europe and America

My [Jewish] friends gave testimony on my behalf to their rabbi. A copy of this document remained with the Jewish Historical [sic] Committee in Krakow, and the other was given to me as my passport to a new life.... It was my friends who took charge of me, who made me one of them and then sent me onward.

—Irena Gut Opdyke

When she regained her strength, Irena searched for her family. But travel was difficult. Poland was a wasteland of destroyed buildings and abandoned death camps. It had been bombed by both the Nazis and the Allies. Unable to find her family, she sought out her Jewish friends in Krakow. Because it had been the Nazi headquarters for all of Poland, Krakow was one of the few cities in Poland that had not been destroyed, and many Jews went there looking for lost relatives. Irena visited the Krakow synagogues left standing to find some of the people she had saved. Excited and grateful to see her, her Jewish friends welcomed her with open arms. They also gave her money to continue her travels.

Based on her past experience, Irena was afraid of the Soviet Russian "liberators"—and rightly so. The Soviets regarded Polish partisans as opponents of the new communist regime in Poland, even though they had previously fought on the same side against the Nazis. As she continued her journey, she was captured by Soviet Russian police, interrogated, and arrested for being a Polish, non-communist partisan. She managed to escape and returned to Krakow to her Jewish friends. They had become her family and now helped *her* to survive. She dyed her hair black to pass as Jewish, and they provided her with a transit pass under the name of Sonja Sierstein. Next, they bought her a train ticket from Soviet Poland to American- and British-occupied West Germany. Holding a document from the Krakow Jewish Committee that verified she had saved Jews, she sought shelter at a DP (displaced persons) camp for refugees in Hessisch-Lichtenau, West Germany. There, she lived for three years among a community of displaced Jewish survivors—a rare occurrence for a Christian woman.

Near the end of 1949, she immigrated to the United States on the troopship *John Muir*, which brought European refugees of many nationalities to America. HIAS, the Jewish resettlement organization, found her a place to live in Brooklyn, New York, and a job in a garment factory. In 1956, she married William Opdyke, a young American who had come to Germany as a United Nations delegate and had interviewed Irena in 1949 at the Hessisch-Lichtenau DP camp. Together, they lived in Yorba Linda, California, where their daughter was born.

Irena led a peaceful life in California, never mentioning that she had saved Jews during the Holocaust. For more than 30 years, she never spoke of her wartime experiences—until 1974 after hearing the lies of a Holocaust denier. Outraged that the Holocaust was being questioned, she confronted him with her own personal story. This motivated her to begin speaking in local churches and synagogues, to community groups, and to high-school students about her experiences. Her mission became to teach young people about the Holocaust, and she traveled widely telling her story.

In 1982, she was honored by Yad Vashem, the World Holocaust Remembrance Center, as a Polish Righteous Among the Nations. Her legacy was affirmed by the Tarnopol Jewish survivors who again gave written testimony of her brave and successful efforts to save their lives. Out of a prewar Jewish population of 18,000, only 200 Jews from Tarnopol had survived. Among them were Fanka Silberman, Henry Weinbaum, Moses Steiner, Marian Wilner, Alex Rosen, David Rosen, Clara Bauer, Thomas Bauer, Abraham Klinger, Miriam Morris, Hermann Morris, Herschl Morris, Pola Morris, Lazar Haller, Ida Haller, and Roman Haller (the baby almost not born)—the Jewish people whose lives Irena had boldly saved.

In Jewish tradition, there is a teaching that if you save one human's life, it is as if you saved the entire world. Irena Gutowna Opdyke displayed the power of one such righteous woman.

Sister Survivors

Ruth Zlotnik Altman

Born December 23, 1914; Died January 6, 2007

Regina Zlotnik Silberstein

Born May 10, 1910 (or December 1, 1907); Died April 15, 1978

I was fearless and foolish, too young to be afraid.

—Ruth Altman

I gave birth to you, my daughter, to make up for those children we lost.

—Regina Silberstein

On a trip to Poland in 1996, Sarah, born after the Second World War to Holocaust survivors, visits the former hometown of her parents. Almost 60 kilometers (37 miles) west of Warsaw, the town of Vishogrod (in Polish, Wyszógrod) is located high on a hill overlooking the Vistula River. Once a picturesque *shtetl*, more than half its inhabitants were Yiddish-speaking Jews before the Holocaust. Today, there is not a single Jew living in the town.

Sarah wants to visit the place of her ancestors, where both her parents were born and raised. On the streets of Vishogrod, by chance, she happens to meet an elderly Christian Polish resident, *Pan* (Mr.) Mieczyslaw Biernat, who knew the families of both her parents before the war. Biernat had been friends with a Jewish boy, Leybl Zlotnik, who lived across the street. Leybl was the younger brother of Sarah's mother, Regina, and her aunt Ruth. As kids, neighbors Mieczyslaw and Leybl played soccer together on the street. During those prewar days, Jewish and Christian children often played together on the streets of Vishogrod, but they never entered each other's homes.

The old man recalls a wartime story about the Zlotnik family. He tells Sarah how, by early 1943, the Nazis had expelled Biernat's family, along with all the other Christian Poles from Vishogrod. Unlike Warsaw, part of the Nazi-occupied General Government region, Vishogrod was part of the district directly annexed into the Nazi Third Reich. This meant that all Vishogrod inhabitants— Jewish *and* Christian Poles—were ousted from the town, to make room for *Volksdeutsche*, ethnic Germans.

One day, "Ruzhka," the sister of Leybl, found the Biernat family in the neighboring town of Legionowo, where the Biernats had resettled. Searching for shelter from the Nazis, desperate Ruzhka begged Biernat's mother to hide her and her sister. The situation for Jews in the Warsaw Ghetto, from where Ruzhka had fled, was becoming intolerable, and they feared being deported to the death camps. Ruzhka's sister, Regina, had money, so they could pay the Biernat family for hiding them. Biernat's mother refused. In Poland, hiding Jews was punishable by death. Instead, she gave Ruzhka some bread and sent her away.

Telling this story to Sarah, Biernat wonders aloud whether the two sisters had managed to survive the Holocaust. Sarah tells him that the two sisters had indeed survived and reveals to him that Ruzhka is her aunt Ruth and that Regina, Ruzhka's sister, is her mother.

◇◇◇

This is the story of Ruth Zlotnik Altman and Regina Zlotnik Silberstein, two ordinary women—sisters, who survived the Holocaust together. Each sister had a role in the other's survival. During the Holocaust, courageous Ruth worked as a courier for the

Jewish underground Resistance in Warsaw. Resourceful Regina had the money to bribe people for food and shelter. They were saved by the audacious bravery of Ruth who connected with Christian Poles, smuggled food, and found hiding places on the Polish Aryan side, outside the Warsaw Ghetto, and by the ingenuity of Regina who covered gold coins in fabric and sewed them into the lining of her coat. While over 300,000 Warsaw Jews died of starvation or disease or were deported to death camps, these two sisters managed to survive in Nazi-occupied Warsaw.

The Story of Two Sisters from a *Shtetl*

Ruth and Regina were two of six children born to Chaye-Sore (Kryse) and Wolf Zlotnik in the *shtetl* of Vishogrod. The two sisters were the only members of their immediate family who survived the Holocaust. The others—their mother, father, two other sisters, two brothers, aunts, uncles, and many cousins—were murdered in Treblinka's notorious death camp in 1942 and 1943.

From the beginning, Ruth and Regina were opposites. Regina was the first-born, a helpful, obedient daughter living with her Orthodox Yiddish-speaking family. Her education ended after the fourth grade, not unusual for observant *shtetl* girls of the time. Instead, she learned household skills from her mother: cooking, baking, sewing, and embroidery. Her "education" came from her experiences later in life.

Ruth was the third child in her family. A rebel from birth, she believed in herself and sought out challenges. Growing up in provincial Vishogrod, Ruth hated the restrictions placed on her. She longed to leave her limited *shtetl* life and craved the big city, where there were better opportunities for young Jewish girls. Most of all, young Ruth wanted to learn a trade so that she could become an independent woman.

Ruth was the first in her family to leave and head to Warsaw. The rest of the family followed years later. In 1929, at age 14, she left Vishogrod to live with an aunt and uncle. In the big city, away from her nuclear family, she thrived. She enrolled at a school run by ORT (Organization for Rehabilitation through Training), an international Jewish institution that offered vocational training and general education for young women in Warsaw. Such schools were popular among urban Jewish women in Eastern Europe in the 1930s. Secular schools enhanced young women's lives and allowed them to better adapt to their Polish environment. In her all-female classes, Ruth learned tailoring, dressmaking, and patternmaking. At ORT, she also studied the Polish language. Many Jews in provincial Poland spoke Polish only as a second language and with a Yiddish accent since Yiddish was their native language. Learning to speak proper Polish, a complex language, would later help Ruth hide her Jewish identity. In prewar Warsaw, she became acculturated to urban life and felt like an equal with the Christian Polish people.

As young women, Regina and Ruth were restricted by their time and place. Each overcame some of the social barriers they confronted as Jewish women. Each of them showed courage in her own way, even before they faced the atrocities of war. In Vishogrod, young Regina fell in love with Yankl Kronenberg, the son of her family's competitor in the flour mill business. When their two families quarreled, Regina's parents stood in the way of their relationship. Regina rejected the formal arranged marriage that her Orthodox community demanded, and she and Yankl became the Romeo and Juliet of their small Jewish community. Around 1937, after the rest of the Zlotnik family relocated to Warsaw—and more important matters, like the fear of Nazi invasion, arose—the couple finally married. Regina had persisted in marrying for love.

In the Warsaw Ghetto

When the Germans invaded Poland on September 1, 1939, everything changed in Warsaw. On September 29, Nazi soldiers entered the city. One of the Nazis' first proclamations was to order all Warsaw Jews to wear armbands with a Jewish star on their upper right arm. Next, Nazis confiscated Jewish property and closed

Jewish businesses, shops, and schools. By October 1940, the Jews of Warsaw—the city with the world's second-largest Jewish population— were ordered to leave their homes and move to a small designated section in the center of the city. All 360,000 Jews, almost one-third of the city's population, were confined to the Warsaw Ghetto, about two and a half square kilometers (just over one square mile). Soon, homeless Jewish refugees from western territories annexed into the Third Reich also crowded into the Warsaw Ghetto. It became the most populated ghetto in all of Nazi-occupied Europe. By mid-November 1940, the Warsaw Ghetto was sealed off by a three-meter (ten-foot) brick wall topped with barbed wire. Nazi guards were posted along its gates. In these cramped quarters, disease spread and thousands died of starvation.

As conditions in the ghetto worsened, there was a desperate need for food and medicine. Jewish women, often as young as 17 or 18, acted as couriers, secretly crossing from the ghetto to the Aryan side of Warsaw. They brought back food and supplies. They also worked as couriers for the Jewish and Polish Resistance and helped obtain forged documents and weapons for these underground groups. Sometimes, they found hidden shelters for Jewish families outside the ghetto and in the countryside.

Ruth became one of those daring young undercover women who smuggled supplies into the ghetto and carried messages to Resistance fighters. Able to pass as a Christian Pole—light haired with high cheekbones and non-Semitic features, and speaking perfect Polish—Ruth bribed the soldiers at the ghetto gates and then boldly walked in the streets of Aryan Warsaw. She went to the city food market, where more Nazi soldiers stood guard, to get supplies for the ghetto. Here, she traded a coat, a skirt, an old pair of shoes, anything she could find in the ghetto, for a loaf of black bread on the black market.

By that time, Regina was married and lived with her husband, Yankl, confined within the walls of the ghetto. Yankl fared better than most others in the ghetto, providing the most essential commodity of all during this time of starvation. He dealt with the production and distribution of bread. Bread was rare and expensive—five times as costly in the ghetto as on the Aryan side of Warsaw. One day, Yankl snuck out of the Warsaw Ghetto. He didn't come home that night, nor the next day, nor the day after. For a long time, Regina refused to give up hope that he would return. But she never saw Yankl again.

By July 1942, the Nazis posted signs announcing that all Jews living in Warsaw would be "resettled" to the east. This was a euphemism for Hitler's plan, the Final Solution, to eliminate the entire Jewish population of Europe. Alongside the posters, a proclamation announced: "All Jews in the Warsaw Ghetto, regardless of age or sex, will be deported. Only those employed in German workshops, the *Judenrat*, the Jewish police, and the Jewish hospital will be exempt."

So began the Great Deportation in Warsaw on July 22, 1942, the beginning of the systemic mass murder of Jews in stages. They were rounded up and herded to *Umschlagplatz*, the Warsaw railway station, for selection. Those who were unproductive, unable to work, were sent on freight trains to the death camps at Treblinka, Majdanek, and Auschwitz. Those who were able to do hard labor were transferred to labor camps outside Warsaw. Those who were needed for work in German-run businesses and factories received a work permit that would keep them "safe" in the ghetto—if only for the time being.

Thanks to her sewing skills, Ruth received a permit to work for a German factory inside the ghetto. There, she met her future husband while they were both forced laborers in a workshop that made caps for Nazi soldiers. A handsome fellow, Martin Altman sat behind attractive young Ruth at the sewing machines. To get her attention, he took out a pair of scissors and cut into the collar of her blouse when no one was looking. In the midst of the terrible events surrounding them, they fell in love.

The second deportation occurred in January 1943, when another 6,000 Jews living in Warsaw were transported or killed. Before the third deportation could happen, a group of young Jewish activists, barely out of their teens, organized an underground armed insurrection that became known as the Warsaw Ghetto Uprising. It was the first and single most important act of armed Jewish resistance during the Holocaust. But the Nazi soldiers were more numerous and better armed. They responded by accelerating their roundups and setting the entire Warsaw Ghetto on fire. By May 1943, the Warsaw Ghetto had burned to the ground, and most of the Jews who did not die from the flames, the smoke, or the shootings were sent to the station at *Umschlagplatz*, where they were forced into the train cars headed to the death camps.

Hiding Underground and Aboveground in Aryan Warsaw

When the Nazis set the ghetto on fire, Ruth, Regina, and Martin escaped together through the smoke-filled streets and into the underground sewer canals. They trudged through excrement up to their ankles until they resurfaced on the Aryan side of Warsaw. Their destination was Sienna Street, where Ruth knew from her Resistance sources of a hidden bunker just outside the ghetto walls where they could temporarily hide.

After two weeks in the Sienna bunker, Ruth found a more permanent asylum for her sister and Martin, the man who would later become her husband. Before they fled the ghetto, she had refused to leave Martin behind and convinced Regina to pay for his way as needed. Ruth contacted the Polish superintendent of the building on the Aryan side of Warsaw where the Zlotnik family had lived in the days before the ghetto. *Pani* (Mrs.) Manyakova, the superintendent, agreed to hide Regina, Martin, and seven other Jewish people in the cellar of 10 Bonifraterska Street for a price. Regina promised to provide the necessary bribes—from the gold coins sewn into the seams of her coat.

Other Jews joined them in hiding. For 13 months, between 9 and 13 people lived in one room in the cellar of 10 Bonifraterska Street. When the superintendent's son-in-law demanded more money, the fugitives knew they were no longer safe. They needed to find a new hiding place.

Ruth said that she had lived aboveground as a Pole during the entire Nazi occupation of Warsaw. Though she secretly worked for the Jewish Resistance, she had many Polish friends who never knew her true identity as a Jew. For four years, she lived under assumed Polish names such as Ruzhka, Zhuta Payaska, or Yadviga. With forged identity papers, she pretended to be a devout Catholic. She went to church each Sunday so she could be seen taking a wafer during communion. In her pocket, she carried a cross to keep herself "safe" and undercover.

After Bonifraterska, Ruth found a safe haven for her sister in *Stare Miasto*, the Old Town section of Warsaw. There, Regina adopted a false identity as a Polish Roman Catholic, born Maria Kowalska in Luck, Poland, and married to a Pole named Jan Zlotnick. Under this alias, she lived at 11 Freta Street where she worked as a cook and housekeeper for a bachelor named Richo. In his apartment, she occupied a small room, almost a closet, off the kitchen. Fearing that her true identity would be discovered, she rarely left the flat. A lone woman living with a male stranger, surrounded by Polish neighbors who might turn her in—it must have been a frightening experience.

The two things Regina later recounted about Richo was that he had a wart on his nose and that he owned a parrot. She often told the story of how, one day, his beloved parrot bit the wart off his face. When the shocked man screamed, she was afraid that the noise might attract the attention of their Polish neighbors or the Nazi soldiers patrolling the street. Never did Regina elaborate any further about her experience of living alone with Richo. Many years later, her "amusing" story about the parrot and the wart must have covered up her trauma and her true feelings about this terrifying time in her life.

Regina lived in Richo's flat in the Old Town until the Polish Warsaw Uprising. This citywide rebellion against the Nazi occupiers, led by the underground Polish Home Army, began on August 1, 1944. Receiving no help from the Soviet army, supposedly their ally—now stationed across the Vistula River from Warsaw—the Polish rebellion was unsuccessful. In retaliation, the Nazis killed thousands of Warsaw citizens and bombed the city. Those left alive fled to the streets from burning buildings. On orders from the top, Nazi soldiers were instructed to capture all Polish civilians and deport them to Nazi concentration camps in Germany to work as forced laborers. It is probable that Regina was rounded up in the Old City when it fell into Nazi hands on September 2, 1944. She was among the many women deported to Germany as a Christian Polish prisoner—not as a Jew.

German documents show that Regina, alias "Maria Regina Zlotnicka, born Kowalska, prisoner number 35526," was captured by the Nazis on September 2, 1944, and sent to Auschwitz two days later. On September 18, she was briefly transferred to Ravensbrück, the women's concentration camp in Germany, and from there, on October 29, 1944, she reached her destination as a forced laborer at a Buchenwald subcamp in Meuselwitz, Thuringia, near the German city of Leipzig. According to camp registration forms, she was deported from camp to camp with no personal possessions. No longer did she have the gold coins in her lining to bribe her way to safety—she didn't even own a coat.

Regina (alias Maria) was among 271 Polish women sent to Meuselwitz. By January 1945, the labor camp held 1,666 prisoners, of which 1,376 were female. Women provided forced labor for the munition factory, which produced small rocket launchers and grenades for the Nazis. Females were preferred for this job since their smaller hands were more adept at handling tiny parts. They also received less payment for their work than their male counterparts. On a December 1944 "Prisoners' Money and Reward" list for inmates, it stated that Prisoner 35526, Maria Zlotnicka, received four *Reichsmark* (equivalent to less than two dollars at the time) for her labor that month.

In April 1945, when the Nazis were close to losing the war, they evacuated many of their labor camps to hide the evidence of their horrific deeds. Munitions factories were vacated and thousands of inmates were forced on death marches before the Allies could reach the camps and view the damage. Many of the inmates died en route, often to unknown destinations. It is not known whether Regina, alias Maria Zlotnicka, was among the marching prisoners. What is known is that she managed to stay alive—and eventually, once the war was over, set free to return to Warsaw.

After the War

Warsaw was in ruins when it was liberated by the Soviet Red Army on January 17, 1945. Two thousand Jewish survivors emerged from underground hideouts and destroyed buildings in the city. Other Jews gradually returned to Warsaw—from the camps, from hiding places in the country, or from exile in the Soviet Union—hoping to find family members or friends. All searched for missing relatives. Returning Jewish refugees registered at the Central Committee of Jews in Poland, hoping to find loved ones who survived. According to documentation in Warsaw's Jewish Historical Institute's archives, Ruth was one of the first Jews to register at the Warsaw Central Jewish Committee as early as January 31, 1945. She had courageously remained undercover in Warsaw throughout the war.

Ruth hadn't heard from Regina since she was deported to Germany, and Ruth grieved that she was the only one left from their large family. After the war, she lived with Martin in a decimated flat above the cellar of a pressing factory on Sienna Street. One day, Ruth looked out their window and saw her sister, emaciated and pale, but alive. Regina had finally made the long, difficult journey back to Warsaw. When they met at the front steps of the building on Sienna Street, the sisters embraced and cried in each other's arms.

Regina lived with Ruth and Martin for several months. With only one pair of shoes between them, the sisters had to decide, each day, which one would leave the flat. One morning in July 1945, Regina's brother-in-law Menachem Silberstein, who had been married to her husband Yankl's sister, appeared at their door. Menachem had returned from Mauthausen, the last concentration camp to be liberated by the Allies, and found Regina's name listed at the Central Jewish Committee in Warsaw as being alive. The former in-laws fell into each other's arms, grateful to have found each other. Finding any family member alive was reason for rejoicing. When they acknowledged that neither of their former spouses would return, Regina and Menachem decided to marry. Courtship and romance were no longer on the agenda; their love would grow with time.

In less than a year, Ruth and Regina, with their husbands, left Poland for the last time. They fled westward—first to occupied Berlin, their transitional home for several years, then to the United States of America.

The Sisters in America

Ruth and Regina rarely spoke about their Holocaust experiences. And when they did, they couldn't agree on the finer points of their recollections. As bonded as the two sisters were by their experiences during the war, they continued to be opposites in their new lives in the United States. When she immigrated to America as a refugee, Ruth lived in urban New York City. Regina and her husband bought a 40-acre chicken farm in rural Connecticut and tended to 5,000 chickens.

Ruth wanted to forget the past and become an American. When she and her husband immigrated to the United States, all her energy went into creating a new life. From Germany, Ruth and Martin sailed to Galveston, Texas, where their ship, the USS *General Stewart*, docked in November 1949. Convinced that Texas was not the place for them, Ruth and Martin took the long train ride north to New York City, where they rented a small basement apartment on the Upper West Side. There they began their tailoring business, which led to a cleaning and alterations shop on Third Avenue between 64th and 65th Streets in Manhattan, a short walk from the elite Bloomingdales department store.

With her old-school European training as a seamstress and

patternmaker and her innate talent, Ruth developed a successful custom-made couturier business. She went from being a lowly sewing machine operator in a Nazi factory to becoming an appreciated, well-paid fashion designer. Charming her wealthy Manhattan clients with her superb craftsmanship and refined European accent and manners, she created garments from expensive French fabrics— silks, brocade, crepe, gabardine—often copied from the current season's Paris fashion magazines. Crepe blouses, fine woolen suits, flowing silk and taffeta gowns cut on the bias—these creations flowed from her agile fingertips. In the early 1960s, she was one of the first to get a dishwasher in order to save those delicate hands.

On their immigration documents, Martin had been listed as "tailor," while Ruth was "housewife." In reality, it was Ruth who had the skills, talent, and aptitude to run the business—and she became the breadwinner for their household. Unlike her sister Regina, Ruth never had children, but she passed on her flair, her independent spirit, and her business acumen to others. She encouraged younger women who worked in her shop—refugees like herself—to learn their craft and go into business for themselves.

Ruth always knew how to survive. Just as she had once learned to speak impeccable Polish, she took English classes to perfect her English. And just as she had left the *shtetl* for better opportunities in the big city, she was determined to integrate into urban life in New York City. She made American friends on the beach in Coney Island and ate shellfish with them at Chinese restaurants—just as she had cultivated friendships with Christian Poles in Aryan Warsaw.

Meanwhile, Regina's life in rural Connecticut revolved around her home, her husband, and her daughter. Never comfortable speaking English with Americans, she surrounded herself with fellow Jewish survivors. Regina became the lynchpin that held a group of friends—all Holocaust survivors—together. Because they had few blood relations, friends became family. For Jewish holidays, everyone gathered around Regina's table, elegantly set with a white tablecloth, Rosenthal gold-rimmed dishes, and European sterling cutlery.

At her table, every meal began with the aromatic golden liquid that represented health and celebration in her home: chicken soup. Regina may have skimped on details about her life, but she never skimped on the ingredients of her soup. Into her pot, she dropped the mandatory neck, heart, and gizzard, adding several plump chicken feet for flavor. When they were available, she bought *eyerlekh*, premature egg yolks—early embryos—taken from the cavity of the chicken by the local butcher. The color of amber, these were particularly delectable additions to the soup with their sweet, buttery taste. They were a reminder of her own mother's home in Vishogrod, where young Regina had learned to cook.

When she died, Regina left behind a glass mason jar. Inside, hidden like a secret, were her treasures: recipes for all her favorite dishes and baked goods. They were written on small scraps of paper in her careful hand, some in Yiddish, others in Polish, and still others in broken English.

◊◊◊

Extreme times can make heroines of ordinary people. Ruth and Regina represent the many Jewish women survivors who are unsung heroines. If not for their harrowing experiences after the Nazi invasion, they might have been ordinary young women living normal lives. Both Zlotnik sisters had the strength, the resilience, and the luck to remain alive under horrific circumstances. As well as their resistance during the war years, it was their unflinching determination to carry on with their lives *after* the Holocaust atrocities that made them heroines.

Many women survivors stated that their greatest achievement was bearing healthy children after their physical deprivations and tortures during the Holocaust. Regina gave birth to her first and only child, Sarah, when she was 40 years of age, much older than most new mothers of her generation. Having escaped the brutality of the Holocaust, she bore a child out of her belief in the future.

Ruth and Regina were determined to live fully after the war to make up for all their suffering and losses. Using their well-honed survival skills and their natural inclinations, the two sisters embodied the continuation of Jewish life after the Holocaust.

Author's Note

The idea behind this book began with my mother, Regina Zlotnik Silberstein, and my aunt, Ruth Zlotnik Altman, the "sister survivors" between these covers. I wanted to retell their stories, but I didn't have many facts about their Holocaust years. I knew so little about their wartime experiences—they rarely spoke about them—though these experiences followed them and shaped their lives. And mine. A lot of interviewing and research followed, much of it years after their deaths.

When my mother died, I was in my twenties. I had given birth to my first child, Rebecca, the year before. Several years after my mother's death, my second daughter, Hannah, was born. I considered Rebecca and Hannah the "sisters of the future," while I was the generation in-between—the link between these two sets of sisters. I wanted to carry forward my mother's and my aunt's stories of resilience so that their traumatic experiences, their tragic losses, and their notable courage during and after the Holocaust would be remembered by my daughters' generation and thereafter.

After years of working on other people's books, it was time to write my own. With my mother's and my aunt's spirits perching on my shoulders, I wanted to convey the lives of other women who lived courageously through the Holocaust years and after—to tell their often-forgotten stories. As I searched for women to write about, there were many, many heroines to choose from. I finally selected seven other women, some of whom had special meaning in my life.

How did I come to choose these women? As a preadolescent and young teenager, I had spent several years in West Berlin with my parents in a community of Eastern European Jewish survivors, living among the Germans. It was in Berlin that I celebrated my bat mitzvah, said to be the first in Berlin since the end of the war. In researching this book, I found it fitting to delve into Jewish feminist history in Berlin before the Second World War—and yes, it did exist. To my surprise, what I discovered was the little-known story of the first ordained woman rabbi, Rabbi Regina Jonas, ordained in Berlin and murdered in Auschwitz. Her story opens this book.

The rest of the unsung heroines profiled in this book are women who *survived* the Holocaust. I specifically chose the stories of women survivors because they represent the voices of those who gave life to the future. They made bold decisions and carried out courageous acts that helped them stay alive. They also embraced the challenges of creating a new and meaningful existence in the aftermath of war.

Years ago, I was fortunate to work as editor and co-writer with survivor Faye Schulman, whose book, *A Partisan's Memoir*, described her life as a young Jewish female member of a Soviet partisan brigade. I first heard her speak publicly to an audience in Toronto in 1993. She was a photographer who became a nurse and a partisan guerilla fighter during the Second World War, all the while taking photographs to document her wartime experiences. She used these photos in her slideshow, displaying partisan life in the forests and swamps of Belarus. Even without her photos, her dramatic story is worth retelling in this book.

One of the two non-Jewish women profiled in this book, Irena

Gut Opdyke, was a friend of my family, and I remember her well from my childhood on our Connecticut chicken farm. At the time, I knew nothing of her heroic past. Much later, after her death, I read her memoir, *In My Hands*, and saw the Broadway play, *Irena's Vow*, based on her life. Both were surprising and inspirational to me.

While editing an English-language volume of the Ringelblum Archive for the Jewish Historical Institute in Warsaw, I developed a deep affinity for Rachel Auerbach, a prolific Polish and Yiddish writer and journalist who survived the Holocaust. In her writings, she intimately describes life in the Warsaw Ghetto as my mother and my aunt might have experienced it. Her communal soup kitchen in the ghetto at 40 Leszno Street was on the same street as my mother's ghetto address at 56 Leszno. Like my mother and aunt, she later escaped to the Aryan side of Warsaw.

Unlike my mother and my aunt, who rarely spoke about the Holocaust, Rachel Auerbach believed in the importance of personal storytelling. In her work at Yad Vashem, her mission was to collect firsthand testimonies from Holocaust survivors and to document evidence for those who did not survive. Visiting Israel, my parents contributed to her collections at Yad Vashem with details of the lives and deaths of their own deceased loved ones.

Like Rachel Auerbach, I believe in the power of storytelling. I have been privileged to learn the remarkable stories of these daring heroines and to narrate them in this book. Recent surveys show that many young people today know very few facts about the Holocaust. Some are even unaware that the genocide of six million Jews occurred less than a century ago. With the passing of most living witnesses to the Holocaust, I take seriously my role in forging a link between past and future generations. There is an echo from the past in the present.

I offer this book to the next generation to remind them of the history of the Holocaust by evoking the lived narratives of these nine heroic women. And, like the women in this book, I am committed to understanding the lessons of the Holocaust through my female gaze.

Selected Timeline

January 1933:

- Adolf Hitler appointed chancellor of Germany, marking the end of the democratically elected Weimar Republic and the beginning of the Nazi Party's rise to power. Hitler becomes Germany's autocratic *Führer* (leader) of the Third Reich (Nazi Germany) within a year.

March 1933:

- First concentration camp opened in Dachau, Germany, established as a work camp for political prisoners and Jews. Becomes a prototype for other concentration camps.

September 1935:

- Nuremberg Race Laws enacted by the Nazi Party, giving priority to those of the racially pure "superior Aryan race" and revoking German citizenship from Jews and other minorities. Marriage between individuals of different "races" is forbidden.

November 1936:

- Nazi Germany and Japan sign an alliance.

March 1938:

- Nazi Germany invades and annexes Austria as part of the Third Reich.

November 1938:

- On *Kristallnacht* (night of broken glass), violent anti-Jewish pogroms take place throughout Germany and Austria, marking a violent turning point for the persecution of Jews.

August 1939:

- Germany and Soviet Russia sign the Nazi-Soviet Non-Aggression Pact, with a secret plan to invade and divide Poland.

September 1939:

- Nazi Germany invades Poland from the west, marking the beginning of the Second World War.
- Soviet Russia invades Poland from the east. Soviet Russia and Nazi Germany divide up conquered Poland between them.
- Great Britain and France declare war on Germany.
- Nazi soldiers occupy Warsaw.

May 1940:

- Auschwitz concentration camp established in Poland.
- Nazi troops invade France.

June 1940:

- Soviet Russia invades Lithuania, along with Latvia and Estonia.

September 1940:

- Japan, Germany, and Italy sign the Tripartite Pact to officially form the Axis Powers.

October 1940:

- Nazis establish the Warsaw Ghetto. All Warsaw Jews are forced to leave their homes and move into the ghetto.

November 1940:

- Nazi authorities order the Warsaw Ghetto to be sealed off. All Jews imprisoned within its walls.

June 1941:

- Nazi Germany violates the Nazi-Soviet Non-Aggression Pact and invades Soviet Russia.
- Nazi Germany occupies Kovno, Lithuania.

July 1941:

- Kovno ghetto established, and the massacre of Jews begins.

September 1941:

- Tarnopol ghetto established.

November 1941:

- Theresienstadt "showcase" camp established.
- Belzec death camp established.
- Lvov ghetto established.

December 1941:

- United States enters the Second World War.

January 1942:

- Policy plans for the Final Solution confirmed at the Wannsee Conference by high-ranking Nazi officials. The plan is for the mass murder of all Jews of Germany and Nazi-occupied Europe.

March 1942:

- Nazi deportation of Jews from Lvov ghetto to Belzec death camp.

July 1942:

- Nazi roundups and deportations of Jews from the Warsaw Ghetto to the death camps begin.

August 1942:

- Nazi deportations of Tarnopol Jews to the death camps begin.

January 1943:

- Second deportation of Jews from the Warsaw Ghetto.

April 1943:

- Warsaw Ghetto Uprising, organized by young Jewish fighters, begins. This is the first and largest armed Jewish resistance to the Nazi occupiers during the Holocaust.

May 1943:

- Warsaw Ghetto Uprising defeated by the Nazis. Warsaw Ghetto is destroyed and the remaining Jews are deported to Treblinka and Majdanek death camps.

June 1944:

- D-Day. Allied British, Canadian, and U.S. troops land in Normandy, France. Nazi army begins its retreat from Western Europe.

July 1944:

- Soviet Russian Army liberates Belorussia (White Russia) from the Nazis.

August 1944:

- Unsuccessful Warsaw Polish Uprising begins, led by underground Polish Home Army against the Nazi occupiers.

September 1944:

- Nazi aircrafts bomb Warsaw in response to the Warsaw Polish Uprising and begin deportation of Warsaw civilians to concentration camps in Germany.

October 1944:

- Last transport of Jews from Theresienstadt to the gas chambers of Auschwitz.

January 1945:

- Withdrawal of Nazi troops from the city of Warsaw, and liberation by Soviet Russian troops.

April 1945:

- Adolf Hitler dies by suicide.

May 1945:

- Unconditional Nazi surrender to the Allies.

Map of featured locations

Baltic Se

Ravensbrück **X**

Germany Berlin ●

Netherlands

Hessisch-Lichtenau
👪 Meuselwitz

X

Belgium ● Cologne

X
Buchenwald

X
Theresienstadt

Luxembourg ● Prague

Bohemia
(Czech Republi

● Paris Natzweiler **X**

Danube River

Landsberg am Lech
👪

France **Austria**

👪 Displaced Persons Camp (Post-World War II)

● City or Town

X Concentration Camp

— River

— Borders (2022)

Glossary

Allied Powers: A military coalition during the Second World War that included Great Britain and its Commonwealth nations, France, the Soviet Union, the United States, and other countries opposed to Adolf Hitler. In opposition to the Axis Powers.

Aryan race: In Nazi racial language, the "superior" people from the Nordic countries originating from Germany. Different from the Jewish "race."

Aryan side (of Warsaw): The districts of the city of Warsaw outside the ghetto, not open to Jews.

Ashkenazi Jews: Jews from Europe said to originate from medieval Germany, with similar culture and traditions.

Auschwitz: The largest Nazi death camp in Poland, located near Krakow.

Axis Powers: A military coalition during the Second World War that included Germany, Italy, Japan, Hungary, Romania, and Bulgaria. In opposition to the Allied Powers.

bat mitzvah: A coming-of-age ceremony for Jewish females. Equivalent to a bar mitzvah for males.

Belzec: A Nazi death camp where up to 500,000 Jews were murdered, third after Auschwitz and Treblinka in number of murdered Jews. Only seven people imprisoned there are known to have survived the Second World War.

Berlin Wall: A guarded barrier constructed in August 1961, during the Cold War, by the Soviet East German government (GDR), cutting off West Berlin from surrounding East Germany and keeping East Germans from fleeing to West Germany. A symbol of the Cold War, it was dismantled in November 1989 by East German demonstrators demanding more freedom, forcing the end of the USSR soon thereafter.

black market: The illegal buying, selling, and trading of scarce commodities, especially active in difficult economic times.

concentration camps: Brutal prison camps established by Nazi Germany beginning in 1933 to imprison and punish those considered a threat to the Nazis. Many became death camps, equipped with gas chambers for mass murders.

the Cold War: From 1945 to 1989, an intense economic, political, and ideological conflict between the Soviet Union and the western world, particularly the United States, involving threats and propaganda but stopping short of armed warfare.

Dachau: The first concentration camp established in Germany as a work camp for political prisoners and Jews. Became a prototype for other concentration camps.

DP (displaced persons) camps: Communal living quarters set up by the Allied Powers for Jewish refugees in Germany and Austria after the war.

the Final Solution: Adolf Hitler's premeditated plan for the genocide of all European Jewry, his answer to the "Jewish question," as confirmed by the Wannsee Conference in January 1942.

genocide: The organized elimination of an entire race or ethnic group of people by murder.

the General Government: Administrative region of Poland controlled by the Nazi military after the 1939 invasion. Separate from parts of Poland annexed by Nazi Germany as part of the Third Reich. Composed of central and southern Poland including Warsaw, Krakow, Lvov, western Ukraine, and eastern Galicia.

German Democratic Republic (GDR): East Germany under communist rule from shortly after the Soviets liberated parts of Nazi Germany and until the fall of the Berlin Wall and the USSR, 1945–89.

German reunification: After the fall of the Berlin Wall in November 1989, the process in which East Germany (the German Democratic Republic) and the Federal Republic of West Germany were reunited as one nation in 1990.

Gestapo (Geheime Staatspolizei) [German]: The Nazi secret state police whose main responsibility was to track down and arrest Jews.

ghetto: An enclosed area of a city, often referred to as where Jews were forcibly confined to live during the Holocaust.

the Great Deportation: The beginning of several Nazi roundups and selections of Jews in Warsaw on July 22, 1942, transporting them to the death camps of Treblinka and Majdanek.

the Great War: Name given to the First World War, before the Second World War occurred.

halakhah **[Hebrew]:** The body of Jewish law and tradition comprising the laws of the Bible, the oral laws as transcribed in the Talmud, and subsequent legal codes as interpreted by the rabbis.

HIAS: Formerly the Hebrew Immigrant Aid Society, an American Jewish non-profit resettlement organization that assisted Jewish refugees after the Holocaust and helped them build new lives. Today, it assists refugees of many backgrounds forced to flee their home countries because of persecution or war.

the Holocaust: The systematic, state-sponsored persecution and murder of six million European Jews by the Nazi German regime and its allies and collaborators during the Second World War. The Holocaust was precipitated in January 1933, when Adolf Hitler and his Nazi Party came to power in Germany, and ended in May 1945, when the Allied Powers defeated Nazi Germany.

interwar years: The years between the First and Second World Wars, usually referring to Europe between 1919 and 1938.

the Joint: An American Jewish global humanitarian organization that helped Jewish refugees in the twentieth century. Today, the American Jewish Joint Distribution Committee responds to humanitarian emergencies around the world.

Judenhäuser **(pl.) [German]:** The forced housing for Jews imposed by the Nazis in Germany with several Jewish families per apartment, often one room per family.

kaddish **[Hebrew]:** The Jewish prayer recited in daily ritual by mourners in private or at public services after the death of close relatives or loved ones.

kibbutz **[Hebrew]:** A communal, egalitarian, rural settlement set up in Palestine/Israel before and after Israel's establishment as a state.

Kristallnacht **(Night of Broken Glass) [German]:** The countrywide pogroms of November 9–10, 1938, in towns and cities throughout Germany and annexed Austria.

Majdanek: A death camp in Poland near Lublin.

Nazi (National Socialist German Workers) Party: The autocratic, fascist political party led by Adolf Hitler that controlled Germany from 1933 to 1945.

Nazi-Soviet Non-Aggression Pact: The agreement signed by Nazi Germany and the Soviet Union on August 23, 1939. It divided Eastern Europe into German and Soviet territories and guaranteed that Germany and Russia would not attack each other.

Nuremberg Race Laws: The Nazi laws enacted in September 1935 that defined who was a Jew, dissolving citizenship and human rights for Jews and other minorities in Germany. These laws took away religious rights, restricted Jewish education and public education for Jews, and outlawed intermarriage between "races."

Nuremberg Trials: The postwar international war crime trials conducted by the Allied Powers prosecuting and convicting Nazi war criminals guilty of crimes against humanity that had taken place during the Second World War. Refers to military tribunals that began in Nuremberg, Germany, in November 1945 and ended in October 1946.

ORT (Organization for Rehabilitation through Training): An international Jewish educational institution offering vocational training and general education, especially for young women. Established at the beginning of the twentieth century and still existing today. Women's early support of ORT reflected Jewish women's emergence into public life by creating their own organizations to meet community needs.

***Ostjuden* (pl.) [German]:** Jews from Eastern Europe, typically religious and Yiddish-speaking.

***Oyneg Shabes* [Yiddish]:** The code name for a secret group, headed by historian Emanuel Ringelblum, of writers, teachers, students, economists, and community leaders who wrote and collected thousands of pages of accounts of the final years of Jewish life in Nazi-occupied Poland. Known as the Ringelblum Archive, these accounts included testimonies, memoirs, letters, posters, leaflets, official announcements, and correspondence in Yiddish, Polish, Hebrew, and German.

partisans: Members of armed guerilla groups formed to fight against occupying forces, particularly in enemy-occupied countries. During the Second World War, there were many partisan groups who fought the Nazis from sheltered camps in the forests of Eastern Europe.

pogrom: An attack on a specific ethnic group, in particular that of Jews in Russia or Eastern Europe in late nineteenth and early twentieth centuries, and later in Nazi Germany. *Kristallnacht* is an example of a pogrom.

the Resistance: Secret guerilla groups that fought Nazi occupation during the Second World War. The Resistance included underground Jewish fighters and smugglers in Eastern Europe (as in the Warsaw Ghetto Uprising) and Jewish rebellions that took place in some concentration camps. Hidden in forests in Eastern Europe and in exile, the Polish and Russian partisan Resistance fought outside urban centers. The French Resistance was forced underground by the Nazi Vichy government.

Righteous Among the Nations: Award given by Yad Vashem, the World Holocaust Remembrance Center in Jerusalem, Israel, to non-Jewish individuals who risked their lives to save Jews during the Holocaust. Recipients of the award are often called Righteous Gentiles.

Righteous Gentiles: Non-Jews who risked their lives to save Jewish people from Nazi persecution during the Holocaust. The designation given to those honored as Righteous Among the Nations by Yad Vashem, the World Holocaust Remembrance Center in Israel.

Ringelblum Archive: The most important record of the Jewish experience in Poland during the Holocaust. Initiated by Dr. Emanuel Ringelblum in November 1940, it contains thousands of documents collected and saved about everyday Jewish life in Poland during the Second World War. Buried in 1943 and recovered in two batches in September 1946 and December 1950, the existing original documents are stored in Warsaw by the Emanuel Ringelblum Jewish Historical Institute, which has published many of the documents in Polish and English.

Roma/Romani: An Indo-Aryan ethnic group, once called "gypsies." Like the Jews, they were persecuted and murdered by the Nazis.

semikhah [**Hebrew**]: Ordination to become a rabbi.

shtetl [**Yiddish**]: A small pre-Holocaust town or village in Eastern Europe in which a significant percentage of the inhabitants were Jewish and Yiddish-speaking and lived according to their own religious traditions.

SOE (Special Operations Executive): A British secret intelligence organization specializing in espionage and sabotage. Established by the British government to assist the underground French Resistance after the Nazis invaded France in May 1940.

Soviet bloc: An alliance of countries under Russian Soviet domination from 1945 to 1991, especially those communist countries in Eastern and Central Europe, such as Poland and East Germany.

Soviet Russia/Soviet Union: Formerly the Union of Soviet Socialist Republics, a federation of communist republics that occupied the northern half of Asia and part of Eastern Europe, with its capital in Moscow. After the Second World War, it emerged as a superpower that rivaled the United States and led to the Cold War.

the SS (*Schutzstaffel*) [German]: The elite combat branch of the Nazi Party. First served as personal bodyguards for Chancellor Adolf Hitler.

***tanka* [Japanese]:** A short, five-line traditional Japanese poem similar to haiku.

Theresienstadt: A concentration camp in occupied Czechoslovakia set up by the Nazis as a "model" Jewish town, a fake "showplace" to deceive the rest of the world about Nazi treatment of Jews. Many renowned German Jews were sent there before they were deported to the Auschwitz death camp.

Third Reich (Third Empire): The Nazi regime from 1933 to 1945, so named by Adolf Hitler to refer to Nazi Germany and its annexed territories.

Trans-Siberian Railway: A network of railways connecting Western Russia to the Russian Far East. The longest railway line in the world, running from Moscow to Vladivostok on the Sea of Japan. The route most widely used to travel from Europe to Japan and China during the Second World War.

Treblinka: A Nazi death camp, second to Auschwitz in the number of murdered Jews.

Tripartite Pact: An agreement between Germany, Italy, and Japan signed on September 27, 1940. A defensive military alliance that was eventually joined by Romania and other Eastern European countries aligned with the Nazis, such as Hungary, Bulgaria, Yugoslavia, and Slovakia.

Umschlagplatz **[German]:** The holding area adjacent to railway stations in occupied Poland where Jews from ghettos were assembled for deportation to the Nazi death camps. Usually refers to the *Umschlagplatz* in Warsaw next to the Warsaw Ghetto, the largest collection point in Poland during the Holocaust.

Untermenschen **(pl.) [German]:** People considered racially or socially inferior. A Nazi term for non-Aryan "inferior" people such as Jews, Slavs (Poles), Roma, Africans, and other "ethnic/racial" groups.

USSR (Union of Soviet Socialist Republics): A former union of multiple national republics with a centralized government in

Russia. A federation of communist republics, it existed from 1922 until it was dissolved in 1991.

Volksdeutsche (pl.) [German]: People of German ethnic origin long settled in a central or east European country, repatriated for political reasons by the Nazi regime.

Warsaw Ghetto Uprising: The final act of armed rebellion by young Jewish fighters in the Warsaw Ghetto against Nazi Germany's efforts to transport the remaining Jewish population to the Majdanek and Treblinka death camps. The fighting began on April 19, 1943, and lasted until May 16, 1943 when the Nazis burned the ghetto to the ground.

Warsaw Polish Uprising: The citywide rebellion led by the underground Polish Home Army against the Nazi occupiers. The fighting began on August 1, 1944. Different from the Jewish Warsaw Ghetto Uprising in April 1943.

Wehrmacht [German]: The armed forces, the army, navy, and air force, of Nazi Germany, 1935–45.

Yad Vashem (World Holocaust Remembrance Center): Israel's official memorial museum located in Jerusalem, documenting and honoring the memory of Jewish Holocaust victims and Righteous Gentiles who saved Jews at their own peril. First established by Israeli law in 1953 by the Holocaust Martyrs' and Heroes' Remembrance Authority.

yeshiva: An Orthodox school for talmudic and other Jewish religious studies.

Yiddish: The language spoken widely by Jews in Eastern Europe before the Holocaust.

Yizkor **[Hebrew]:** A public memorial prayer service observed by the community, usually held in a synagogue, for deceased family members and martyrs. It is recited four times a year during Jewish high holidays.

Yizkor **books:** The memorial books of lost Jewish communities in Eastern Europe created after the Holocaust by survivors of those communities.

Zionism: An international movement founded in 1897, in Switzerland by Theodore Herzl, dedicated to creating an official homeland in Palestine/Israel initially for persecuted Jews.

Suggested Reading

Rabbi Regina Jonas

Elisa Klapcheck, *Fräulein Rabbiner Jonas: The Story of the First Woman Rabbi*, translated by Toby Axelrod (John Wiley & Sons, 2004).

Sandy Eisenberg Sasso, *Regina Persisted: An Untold Story*, illustrated by Margeaux Lucas (Berman House, 2018).

Faye (Faigel) Lazebnik Schulman

Faye Schulman with Sarah Silberstein Swartz, *A Partisan's Memoir: Woman of the Holocaust* (Second Story Press, 1995).

Joanne Gilbert, *Women of Valor: Polish Jewish Resisters to the Third Reich* (Adira Press, 2012).

Yukiko Kikuchi Sugihara

Yukiko Sugihara, *Visas for Life*, translated by Hiroki Sugihara (Edu-Comm Plus, 1995).

Ken Mochizuki, *Passage to Freedom: The Sugihara Story*, illustrated by Dom Lee (Lee & Low Books, 1997).

Marc E. Vargo, *Women of the Resistance: Eight Who Defied the Third Reich* (McFarland, 2012), pp. 106–123.

Rachel (Rokhl) Eiga Auerbach

Samuel D. Kassow, *Who Will Write Our History?* (Indiana University Press, 2007).

Rachel Auerbach, "Yizkor, 1943," in *The Literature of Destruction: Jewish Responses to Catastrophe*, ed. David Roskies (Jewish Publication Society, 1988), pp. 459–64.

To date, English translations of sections of Auerbach's work have been published only in specialized journals. They include the following:

Pakn Treger, Summer 2017: "The Librarians," excerpt from Rachel Auerbach's 1974 *Warsaw Testaments*, translated by Seymour Levitan.

Tablet Magazine, May 2016: "Yizkor, 1943."

Bridges Magazine, 2008, "Soup Kitchen, Leszno 40," from the memoirs of Rachel Auerbach, translated by Seymour Levitan.

Rachel Auerbach's Holocaust writings in other languages include the following:

In the Fields of Treblinka (Yiddish), Warsaw, 1947.

The Jewish Uprising: Warsaw 1943 (Yiddish), Warsaw, 1948.

Our Reckoning with the German People (Yiddish), Tel Aviv, 1952.

In the Streets of Warsaw, 1939–1943 (Hebrew), Israel, 1954.

The Warsaw Ghetto Uprising (Hebrew), Israel, 1963.

Warsaw Testaments: Encounter, Activities, Fates, 1933–1943 (Yiddish), 1974; (Hebrew), 1985.

On the Final Road: In the Warsaw Ghetto and on the Aryan Side (Yiddish), 1977.

Vera Rosenberg Atkins

Sarah Helm, *A Life in Secrets: Vera Atkins and the Missing Agents of World War II* (Little, Brown, 2005).

William Stevenson, *Spymistress: The Life of Vera Atkins* (Arcade Publishing, 2007).

Marc E. Vargo, *Women of the Resistance: Eight Who Defied the Third Reich* (McFarland, 2012), pp. 7–26.

Lena Kuchler Silberman

Lena Kuchler Silberman, *One Hundred Children*, adapted from the Hebrew by David G. Gross, (Doubleday, 1961).

Lena Kuchler Silberman, *My Hundred Children*, translated by David C. Gross (Dell, 1987).

Lena Kuchler Silberman's writings in other languages include the following:

Mayne Kinder (Yiddish), Paris, 1948.

My Hundred Children (Hebrew), Israel, 1959 (Yad Vashem).

The Hundred [Will Return] to Their Borders (Hebrew), Israel (Schocken, 1969).

My Mother's House (Hebrew), Israel (Schocken, 1985).

Irena Gut (Gutowna) Opdyke

Irena Gut Opdyke with Jennifer Armstrong, *In My Hands, Memories of a Holocaust Rescuer* (Knopf, 1999).

About the Author

Sarah Silberstein Swartz, daughter of Jewish-Polish Holocaust survivors, was born in post-war Berlin, Germany. She is a writer, translator, and award-winning book editor who specializes in Jewish women's studies and Holocaust history as well as literature for young adults, general readers, and scholars. Her work has been published internationally in Canada, the United States, Germany, and Poland. She recently edited the English-language volume of The Ringelblum Archive, *Accounts from the General Government, 1939–1942*, for the Jewish Historical Institute in Warsaw. Sarah is the developmental editor of numerous books in the "Holocaust Remembrance Series for Young Readers" published by Second Story Press, as well as editor-in-chief of the classic *Jewish Women in America: An Historical Encyclopedia* (eds. Paula Hyman and Deborah Dash Moore). She assisted Faye Schulman in writing her memoir, *A Partisan's Memoir: Woman of the Holocaust*. A dual citizen of the United States and Canada, Sarah lived in Canada for over thirty years where she brought up her two daughters. She is currently a Research Associate at the Hadassah-Brandeis Institute at Brandeis University, where she first gave a talk about "Unsung Heroines of the Holocaust." Sarah lives in Boston with her wife and cat, near her beloved three grandsons.